Lifelike Artist Dolls

How-To and Inspiration from Lynn Cartwright's Studio

Lynn Cartwright

Schiffer Publishing Ltd®

4880 Lower Valley Road • Atglen, PA 19310

Other Schiffer Books on Related Subjects:
Polymer Clay Jewelry: The Art of Caning, Mathilde Brun, ISBN 978-0-7643-4456-5
The Art of the Contemporary Doll, Sandra Korinchak, ISBN 978-0-7643-4860-0
Fashion Design Techniques: The Basics and Practical Application of Fashion Illustration, Zeshu Takamura, ISBN 978-0-7643-5047-4

Cover and design by RoS
All photographs by Lynn Cartwright unless otherwise noted.
Type set in Segoe Scrip/ITC Avant Garde Gothic Std

ISBN: 978-0-7643-5477-9
Printed in China

Published by Schiffer Publishing, Ltd.
4880 Lower Valley Road
Atglen, PA 19310
Phone: (610) 593-1777; Fax: (610) 593-2002
E-mail: Info@schifferbooks.com
Web: www.schifferbooks.com

For our complete selection of fine books on this and related subjects, please visit our website at www.schifferbooks.com. You may also write for a free catalog.

Schiffer Publishing's titles are available at special discounts for bulk purchases for sales promotions or premiums. Special editions, including personalized covers, corporate imprints, and excerpts, can be created in large quantities for special needs. For more information, contact the publisher.

We are always looking for people to write books on new and related subjects. If you have an idea for a book, please contact us at proposals@schifferbooks.com.

All art requires courage.

—Anne Wilkes Tucker

Contents

Studio

Concept

Exploring the Creative Process and Original Artist Dolls as Art

Production, Part 1

Understanding Polymer Clay, Creating Armatures, Assembling, and Record Keeping

Production, Part 2

Hands-on Clay Conditioning, Sculpting, Curing, Refining, and Painting

Production, Part 3

Soft Body Armatures, Soft Body Construction, and Assembly

Marketing
Hobby or for Profit

First Aid
What Could Possibly Go Wrong, You Ask?

Gallery

Preface

I found myself chasing a FedEx truck in Bakersfield late one afternoon! If I could only catch the driver and give him my express package, then I would save myself time and miles to the airport and easily make the pressing shipping deadline.

The unsuspecting driver drove very fast and in a circuitous way with me hot in pursuit. He finally stopped in a cul-de-sac at the most enchanting and curious doll shop. After giving him my package, I was compelled to investigate the new find. Inside the shop, many ladies were busy assembling porcelain dolls in various stages, and there was a captivating gallery display of their finished work. I signed up for classes on the spot!

Weeks passed. The urge to create my own dolls from scratch was very compelling. Although the experience of working with dolls from pre-existing molds was fascinating and educational, designing my own dolls would be more gratifying to my artistic nature.

I then signed up for a doll making class in San Luis Obispo, California, that was taught by famous artist Anthony Bulone. He taught porcelain doll sculpting and specialized mold making. Anthony has produced an impressive repertoire of dolls throughout his career, but he is most noted for sculpting the original Barbie doll in 1957. He had patterned Barbie after his stunning late wife Lylis, whom I met at the time. Barbie was an amazing spot-on double to lovely Lylis.

My background and my life's work was in fashion design for well over four decades. Since very early on, I

always knew what I wanted to be…a fashion designer. Everything I did was preparation toward that goal.

I devoured fashion magazines as a young girl, created childhood paper dolls with elaborately designed wardrobes, learned to knit and embroider, and sewed much of my own wardrobe. Later, I attended the University of Minnesota as an art major, then studied a fashion design curriculum in Los Angeles, California, at LA Trade Technical College, Otis, and UCLA. My seventeen years of self-styled education is equivalent to a Bachelor of Arts degree.

I intentionally started from the bottom as a pattern maker and grader (a grader is one who engineers the range of sizes). I wanted to become accomplished at the jobs I would eventually supervise as a designer.

As a California based fashion designer, I designed apparel appropriate to my geographic region—swimwear, surfwear, active sportswear, lifestyle sportswear, etc. California's love of color and the active beach lifestyle predominantly influence the West Coast fashion image. I also briefly designed and manufactured a line of children's dresses and sportswear under my own label— Skippy of California.

Later, as a fashion design consultant servicing manufacturers in the US and in Asia, I designed programs in knitwear, outerwear, active sportswear, athletic footwear, medical, technical and fashion uniforms, fast food programs, etc. I was energized by the product diversity. At one point, I designed seven product lines simultaneously, each having two to four annual seasons!

I am recognized in the apparel industry as transforming medical uniforms with warmhearted and humanizing nurses scrub prints that remain influential today. And, probably my most prestigious design commission is the 1984 and 1988 USGF or United States Gymnastics Federation's Olympic uniform leotards. Recall Mary Lou Retton's patriotic uniform.

A great fringe benefit of my fashion design career was traveling to inspiring and exotic places around the world and experiencing different cultures firsthand. I traveled for both design inspiration and for product development. I made many new friends around the world, and met amazing people who have profoundly influenced my life.

A new door opened for me. Everything I had experienced and done up to this point was seeking a new interpretation and an outlet in doll making. I truly consider doll making to be my autobiography.

Photos courtesy of Anthony Bulone

Acknowledgments

A special thanks to my good friend, Ginny Espinoza, who has the misfortune of also being my next-door neighbor. Thank you for your candor, unending positive support, and especially thank you for figuring out how to make an Asian knot!

Thank you, too, John, my ex-husband, for your enduring encouragement in this book and in all my creative endeavors.

Thank you Jennifer, my lovely talented daughter, for your photography, your modeling, and for just being there.

Introduction

The goal of this book is to provide a window into my particular doll making process, and to celebrate the body of my work.

My methods may be unconventional at times, but all methods and techniques came about through labored hands-on personal experiences, both good and bad ones. Each of my dolls is a blending of idealism and pragmatism.

Surprises occur along the way. Original ideas, more often than not, evolve into something quite different, and the final product may vastly deviate from the original vision.

I marvel over the diversity of original artist dolls from the many talented doll makers throughout the world. Each artist has a unique signature style that unfolds unconsciously during the doll making process, resulting in diversity. Artists put themselves into their art.

There is no benefit in copying another artist's work. The purpose of learning new doll making techniques, like the ones presented here, should facilitate the self-expression of each doll maker and not open a grim door to plagiarize. Please don't go there. There is no happiness or artistic satisfaction in this.

Gallery

The vast body of my work is merchandised into groups or statements that are meaningful to me. This is how I worked as a fashion designer. I made meaningful design statements and groups within each apparel collection.

Especially dear to me are the Native American tribes or nations. The *Born in America* collection is made up of dolls representing various indigenous tribes. I study each tribe's customs and philosophy in order to accurately portray my dolls. Authenticity in their accessories is of utmost importance to me; however, be aware that it comes at a price. This collection is of interest to both collectors of artist dolls and collectors of Native American artifacts.

Other design collections include *Heirloom Portraitures,* or custom portrait dolls, and the *One World* collection, which addresses global cultures and varied ethnicities. *Remarkable Women* recognizes noteworthy women, both contemporary and historical, who have made significant social contributions. *Dolls to the Rescue: Saving Endangered Wildlife* is a newer collection that is self-explanatory by the name. A significant portion of the doll's cost goes toward an applicable charity. Other collections are evident in the Gallery section.

Studio

Concept

Exploring the Creative Process and Original Artist Dolls as Art

CREATIVITY

In Theory

In creating an original handmade artist doll from scratch, let's start from the very beginning—the understanding of the creative process.

According to Wikipedia, creativity is defined as the ability to transcend traditional ideas, rules, patterns, relationships, and the like, and to create meaningful new ideas, forms, methods, interpretations, etc.; originality, progressiveness, and imagination are the result.

I say **does it have a heart?** Start by selecting a doll theme or idea that has a significance or a heart for you. Give this some thought and brainstorm ideas.

Does your doll make a **statement**? Whether it is a portraiture of a loved one, a character doll, or a doll with an underlying message or purpose, your doll does make a statement. A part of that unconscious statement is about you, your values, your skills, and your personality. You intrinsically put yourself into your artwork. The doll's statement should hopefully educate, entertain, and delight collectors and doll makers.

Challenge is an important part of creativity. It is a motivator. It is the beginning of all worthy ideas. It is growth.

Risk-taking is key to success, as scary as it sounds. The challenge of trying something new, or even breaking the rules, may be luring and seductive. Champion your failures if something goes awry. Failures should be looked at as a starting point for new discoveries. Remember that raw clay can happily be recycled and reused in the event of a hopeless sculpting tragedy. I have been there. There is always a second chance and a way out, and sometimes the second chances can lead to a higher success. I call these good surprises.

Establish **boundaries.** Design is facilitated after setting perimeters or boundaries. Having no pre-established perimeters or having total freedom is oddly more challenging and inhibiting than working within pre-established guidelines. Some boundaries include the clay's limitations, available supplies, the doll's scale or size, the artist's skill level, time restraints, and the like. Set your boundaries before beginning the project.

Design flourishes with a fresh new **objectivity.** Especially in the case of designing something new to your skill level, something surprisingly positive can result with a fresh open-minded vision. Revisiting an ongoing project will also have renewed enthusiasm and a restored perspective.

When confronted with a vexing problem, Buddhist monks, rather than acting immediately on it, would let their subconscious mull it over, or even sleep on it. A clear answer would miraculously become known through their subconscious. I have experienced this phenomenon.

Creativity is actually a two part process. It is a dichotomy between **design and craftsmanship,** or a marriage between art and craft. It does not mean that a good artist is a good craftsperson. Both skills require study and lengthy self-education. Some artists are better at craftsmanship and others at aesthetics. I believe design reigns supreme over craftsmanship, but not by much. Here is an experience that prejudiced my opinion:

On one of my New York fashion design business trips, I visited a gallery that displayed a large, stunning, million-dollar Alexander Calder mobile. As an enthusiast of contemporary art, it was truly a treat to me. The gallery's ceiling was standard room height and the mobile was gigantic. It projected low enough to touch and low enough to scrutinize its craftsmanship up close. I was astounded to see the individual shapes of this beautiful work of art so crudely executed. The mobile's shapes looked as though they had been cut or gnawed out with nail clippers, yet the overall look was still quite marvelous. My conclusion was that this was ultimately a stunning work of art, but the craftsmanship was definitely greatly subordinate to its design.

In doll making, we strive for both exceptional design and fine craftsmanship. Both are important ingredients in a successful work of art

A **mentor** to me is someone, i.e., a fellow doll maker, who inspires and teaches through their artistic example. They are wonderful inspirational artists who represent our best ideals and standards in doll art. Benefit by their talent and innovation, but avoid blatant imitation.

Order in your environment frees the mind to create. The feeling of chaos disrupts the flow of creativity and diminishes one's strength and control. Organization is necessary in order to undertake any creative project, even if it is only a gesture to neatly display one's sculpting tools in the work space. Order and harmony in the doll maker's studio is conducive to a positive outcome. When everything is in its place, clean, and accessible, the unencumbered mind is free to focus and unleash imagination and skill.

Temperature and humidity should be favorable for creativity to thrive. Polymer clay works best in controlled temperatures and humidity levels.

I am convinced that an essential part of the creative process is to feel somewhat imperfect. The feeling of **imperfection** means that you have high goals and you care deeply about the results.

This can be a good motivator, encouraging you to do your best.

Many Navajo rug makers have been known to purposefully weave a flaw or deviation from the rug's pattern into their carpets as a declaration of their flawed humanness. It is a testament that humans cannot achieve perfection, and they are not Gods.

The zeal of creativity often compels us to share or talk about our ideas that are in process prior to actualizing them. Some may say that this helps further refine and improve our ideas with the input of others, but I feel that you run the risk of interrupting the creative process and detracting from the project's momentum, as well as your own unique point of view. Are we compelled to share our enthusiasm, or are we insecurely seeking out validation before it is earned? Negative feedback may have a negative impact on the project, and then all may go sour. You may find yourself defending the project, and who needs this? Just **don't talk away your ideas.** Sometimes you can talk away the project, which may result in it never coming to fruition!

A good job takes time. **Allow time** for all steps in the process and don't race. Doll making is NOT a spontaneous activity. Always allow yourself time to succeed and time to fail! It is best to quit a project on a high note. Stop when you feel good about what you've done. When you come back to a project, you will have a fresh eye and a new objectivity to proceed and make strides.

Perfection is knowing when to stop. **Don't overwork** your doll. It will be obvious to you when you know enough is enough. I actually experience a physical feeling that comes over me when it is time to stop.

Surprises occur along the way—both good and bad. Be open to them both. Good surprises are gratifying and self-validating, and bad surprises are hopefully lessons learned and a new optimistic path forward. An artist's sensitivity and emotional readiness are foremost in the process of creative focus and flow. Be open to new ideas.

Focusing on the step-by-step process yields a positive outcome in the final product. To begin a project and feel overwhelmed over trying something new may be unsettling, but it is best to focus on the step-by-step process or **baby steps** to achieve a final result which you can display with pride. Early on in my doll making, my first dolls were sculpted and then cast in porcelain. Looking back, they looked awkward and were very obviously experimental.

A good friend gave me a challenge that I still struggle with today. She said that I need to develop **my own style.** The thought of this was both bewildering and terrifying. What did this mean? My late friend Lee Lentz was a successful businesswoman who owned a doll shop, taught classes in porcelain doll making, and pretty much succeeded at everything she set her mind to. I respected her opinion. As time passed and with more experience, I surmised that this is not something that can be decided, but it was innate. My own particular style comes from the manifestation of my values. It happens subconsciously. I believe that my obsession with quality and authenticity, the quest for realism, my sense of style, my celebration of various ethnicities—especially my interest in Native American cultures, the storytelling and educational aspect, all combined with a good measure of humor and whimsy result in my own style. My fashion design background has been extremely influential, too. Both in methodology and in design approach. All this has created my own recognizable style.

My dolls have become my autobiography.

In Practice

In the apparel industry, there is an established procedure or flow when creating product. **Concept** or product design is first, **Production** follows, then there is **Marketing** at the completion of the product. I carry over this methodology to doll making and treat doll making like a disciplined business. Here is a project checklist to follow when applying this to creating an original handmade artist doll from scratch:

Concept:

1. Brainstorm ideas—do research, collect clippings, make sketches, snip swatches, check out photos, and spend time mulling over ideas
2. Design boards—make a composite of the best ideas or themes on design concept boards with sketches, clippings, swatches, etc.
3. Project basket—accumulate swatches, fabrics, findings, etc. into a dedicated project basket along with the design boards
4. Studio prep:
   a) Organization of workspace environment—clay storage, sculpting tools, clay machines, files and sanding supplies, paints, etc.
   b) Cleanliness of the workspace—make it neat, then make it clean and inviting to creativity
   c) Cost sheets—initiate cost sheets (see template) and preliminary documentation that will be updated throughout the entire project

Production:

1. Armatures—engineer the doll—generate drawings showing assemblage, connections, schematics, etc.; plan ideal armatures for sculpted parts
   a) Doll's head—choose desired head construction type: flanged head, socketed head, head and partial shoulder plate, head and torso, etc.
   b) Doll's appendages/limbs (arms, legs)—choose desired poses and adapt armatures accordingly
   c) Choose support stands for armature components—head, shoulder, appendages used for sculpting and baking *(optional)*
   d) Doll eyes—select appropriate size and color of eyes for the scale of the head (eyes will most likely be baked into sculpted head)
2. Clay supply—inventory clay and organize by dye lots for the project
3. Sculpt
4. Bake
5. Sand and refine
6. Create an armature for soft body torso; sew soft body and assemble doll; stuff body with pellets and fiber fill
7. Paint—face and appendages, all sculpted parts
8. Apply lashes and wig
9. Clothe doll and add props, if any
10. Cost sheet—update and finalize all information on the cost sheet for record-keeping purposes

Marketing:

1. Decide the ultimate purpose of your doll making: a hobby or for profit
2. Price doll: consult cost sheet for basic cost of doll, evaluate labor aspect of doll, and calculate an equitable retail
3. Cost introduce doll to public: trade shows, fairs, and media
4. Always remember to take good photos

ORIGINAL ARTIST DOLLS

Defined

The doll category discussed here is called *Original Artist Dolls.* Some say OOAK, which translates into one-of-a-kinds. Dolls in this category are individually hand-sculpted and are not intended to be duplicated. They are neither offered in small limited editions *(LE)*, nor large production runs, as are dolls generated from production molds. Summed up, each doll is an individual expression of art, and most definitely is not a factory widget.

In my opinion, mass produced dolls in most mediums often come across blank, expressionless, and almost appear to be comatose! Sorry, this is harsh! This occurs because the production process predicates the final visual outcome. In mass production, doll parts must be easily extruded from rigid molds; therefore, dolls' facial features lack lifelike dimension and appear bland, smooth, and compromised.

Currently, there is a movement in doll art toward realism. As a proponent of this movement, I strive for natural realistic appeal in my handmade dolls. One-of-a-kind polymer clay artist dolls offer the best medium to create dolls with realistic features and lifelike expressions. There are no molds involved; therefore, sculptural dimension is limitless.

Dolls seem to be a creative balance between realism and fantasy. Even lifelike doll body proportions may be slightly exaggerated, allowing the artist to take poetic license. The dolls may not be textbook anatomically correct, but this freedom of expression can ultimately add to their mystique.

Because of the static nature of artist dolls, they intentionally may have limited posing ability. Heads and arms can sometimes be posed to a small degree. They are not play dolls, and their clothing is not meant to be removed, nor their hair re-styled. They are lovely images frozen in time as figurative works of art.

The category of dolls called *BJD* or *ball jointed dolls* is currently popular among doll collectors, but I believe that the fragility of cured polymer clay would not be the best workable durable medium for this kind. Other mediums like wood, metal, resins, and vinyls are better suited for the wear and tear this construction technique demands. In addition, BJDs are intended to involve the viewer to participate in posing the doll, thus making them more like play dolls and less like works of art, as they were originally intended.

Both *portrait dolls* and *character dolls* are in the category of original artist dolls. *Portrait dolls* are personalized portraitures of specific people, most often children, created as a doll sculpture. I like to think of portrait dolls as heirloom dolls. They are precious reminders of loved ones past or present, preserved for posterity. In creating my portrait dolls, the subject's own hair is styled into a wig in a favorite typical hairdo, and skin and eye colors are meticulously color matched. Personalized clothing is either sized down for the doll, or similar apparel is specifically created with the desired look.

Photos are useful in referencing the subject. A recognizable expression is recreated to portray the subject's own unique personality. Portrait dolls are the most personal kind of portraiture, I believe.

When creating any artist doll, my goal is to create a doll that will last one hundred years or generations, with proper care.

I educate my collectors about the most successful ways to care for these fragile special dolls in order to extend and ensure their longevity.

Character dolls refer to all other dolls that are not associated with a particular recognizable human subject. My Native American dolls, plus various other ethnicities, are usually included in this group. Novelty dolls are also in this group.

As Art

The buzz from savvy art enthusiasts is that original artist dolls, as a category, is perceived as **a new art form.** It may be a variation or an updating of representational figurative art, and deviates from what we know as traditional sculpture, simply by the fact that the figures wear clothing! If the dolls were cast in bronze, there would be no doubt that it is art to all the traditionalists.

The definition of art varies widely, depending upon whom you ask.

One way to summarize it is as human-made creations that are appreciated for beauty or emotional impact and produced by expressing creativity.

The real question, however, is whether it is *good* art. Original artist dolls follow the same fundamental principals of good art as other art forms, and can be judged by those standards. I believe that this is an individual thing depending upon the particular doll sculpture in question. And, let's face it, there is always more bad art than good in any medium.

Ayn Rand, American novelist and philosopher, best defines good art in her best-selling book *The Romantic Manifesto*. The book is a collection of essays devoted to the nature of art. She states that a good artist abstracts from the real world and makes it into the ideal.

The original artist doll should be designed with idealism in mind. I hope my original artist dolls represent Ayn Rand's image of the ideal. The point at which I feel my dolls are elevated to good art status in my mind, I believe, occurs when the doll takes on a personification or spirit. This can actually happen early on in the sculpting process. It does not surface easily, but you will know when it occurs. It is a feeling. On the flip side, if this does not occur, then it's time to recycle the clay!

The hallmark in doll art is to create a lasting masterpiece of superb craftsmanship and unique artistic self-expression. The work of art emulates a human spirit or soul that touches and enlightens the observer.

Successful artwork has a mystique that stimulates an ongoing sense of wonder and discovery in the onlooker.

The one-of-a-kind doll artwork is intended to be a collector's trophy and not a child's play thing. Because of the fragile nature of the medium, and its inflexible qualities, it should be regarded only as a piece of fine art and cared for as such. In this book it will be termed as *art*.

Design and craft this piece of art with longevity in mind. It is an heirloom that should last at least one hundred years or more, as a time measure. As with most antiques, it will improve with the passing of time, as an antique of the future. Polymer clay dolls have been around for about fifty years, and both painted and unpainted pieces are reported to have endured remarkably well thus far.

The Collectors

Artist dolls take on many roles to collectors. Some collectors are theme focused, i.e., they only prefer Native American dolls, black dolls, fashion dolls, bride dolls, antiques dolls, etc. Portrait dolls are a favorite, too, since they connect one with their heritage or family and give a sense of belonging. A portrait doll can also be a reminder of a lost child and it keeps their memory alive and present. Artist dolls can also take on the role of decorative art. For example, a Native American cradle board baby can be a stunning accent to a collector's luxurious log home. Baby and child dolls are a favorite when there is an empty nest or childless home. An artist doll can add the presence of a life form to a home. Some people collect just because they can, but I'm sure their joy in owning a special doll is no less diminished. They are just more fortunate.

One collector of my work purchased two dolls as special gifts. The first was for her granddaughter. She told me that she wanted her granddaughter to know what a real doll looks like. The other doll was a gracious gift for a cherished longtime employee. Once, I bartered a doll with my lawyer Cindy for legal services. She was a collector of bride dolls, so I created a festive doll that would fit into her bridal collection and named the doll Stefany. Stefany was payment for my divorce from Stefan, you see!

I can only speak from my experience, but I believe that a doll collector will know instantly when they see the doll they love…it's personal. They need no convincing to acquire it. It connects to who they are, and will provide timeless enjoyment. Some dolls just break your heart. I have also been a collector and know the feeling.

One of the responsibilities of a fashion designer is to educate their company about their apparel line and the trends.

I also educate my doll collectors as to the care of precious artist dolls. Along with the *Certificate of Authenticity,* a care instruction sheet is given to educate doll buyers.

POLYMER CLAY

Introduction

Polymer clay originated in Germany in the 1930s, providing many uses at the time. Originally, it was intended to be a safer substitute for Bakelite, an early phenol-base plastic that had flammable properties in its uncured state. It was used to make decorative mosaics, and was even used in limited prosthetics. Polymer clay initially gained interest both in commercial applications and in general arts and crafts areas.

Around 1939, a formulation of polymer clay was given to celebrated German doll maker *Kathe Kruse* for use in her doll factory. It proved impractical for her use, but served as a suitable recreational modeling clay for her young daughter, Sophie, aka Fifi.

In 1964, adult Fifi sold the clay formula to Eberhardt Faber where it was commercially marketed as *Fimo*. It soon gained popularity as a crafting clay for hobbyists. Fimo was initially used for small dolls and miniature dollhouse furnishings and accessories. Today, cured Fimo is reported to be the hardest of the polymer clays, making it a suitable medium for jewelry and beadwork artists.

Today, polymer clays are superior and technically advanced and are widely available to hobbyists. Their time is right as a creative medium.

Through time, the polymer clay formula has undergone subtle changes. Contemporary polymer clay is a modeling clay simply comprised of PVC *(polyvinyl chloride)* resin powder that is suspended in liquid plasticizers. It has hardening properties.

Plasticizers give the clay flexibility. Binders and fillers, like chalks and natural earth clays, add bulk, and color results from pigments.

Although it is called a *clay*, it does not contain typical clay minerals, but it does have gel-like working properties similar to mineral clay.

It responds to the warmth of your hands and is low fired and oven-baked to harden, making it an ideal medium for home crafters.

During baking or curing, the powdered PVC softens in the plasticizer and the particles begin to absorb the plasticizer. Optimally, the particles will eventually fully fuse together and form a solid mass of plastic. Most commercial polymer clay can be conveniently cured in a home oven at temperatures around 265 degrees Fahrenheit.

Commercial polymer clay, marketed for doll making, is available through a number of retailers. It is wise to purchase clay from suppliers who have a consistent clay turnover. This will ensure freshness. Always ask about freshness. Fresh clay is easily pliable. Aged clay requires reconstitution efforts, which disrupts the flow of creativity and may produce undesired results when baked or cured.

It is important to purchase clay with the same lot number, or as I call it *dye lot number*. This number is found on the back of clay packaging. Mixing different dye lots can result in unwanted variations in the cured clay. It is best to prevent unwanted surprises like this and purchase adequate quantities of same-lot-number clay. Purchase a bit more than the project requires. More is better here.

Cernit

Of all my personal experimentation with polymer clays, I favor the *Cernit* brand. But, please understand me, it is not meant for the faint of heart. It requires strength, dedication, and the understanding of this fine medium. And above all, total respect for the clay! But, the results can be absolutely marvelous.

Cernit is more popular in Europe than the US, and the general consensus is that it is the *best* polymer clay available for one-of-a-kind doll making. Cernit, sold in small slices of 50 grams or sizable bricks of 500 grams, offers more than seventy-five different pre-formulated colors, among which is a select range of ethnic skin tones. Custom colors can be mixed by the artist—even skin tones. The final look of cured Cernit is somewhat reminiscent of alabaster.

A more people-friendly doll making polymer clay alternative is *ProSculpt.* It is easily manipulated or worked and may be a good starting point for novices before attempting the Cernit challenge. It was created by a doll artist for doll artists. Currently, the color range is limited to three skin tones plus translucent white. It is especially favored by baby-doll makers. The final cured result is opaque, whereas Cernit is slightly more translucent.

There is a multitude of various polymer clays on the retail market today. Cernit and ProSculpt are my favorite, but many others are noteworthy.

German *Fimo* endures today both in Classic and in Soft formulas. Fimo is most often sold in small 2 oz. / 57 gram bars and is more popular with jewelry sculptors, offering a wide range of colors and textures. *Modelene* is an Australian clay, not easily found in the US. It apparently has similar properties to Cernit and is popular in Australia and Europe. An American clay, *Super Sculpey* is offered in a semi-translucent beige tone plus two other light skin tones in 1-pound bricks, which they recommend blending with Sculpey III's color range of 30 two-ounce bars for custom tones.

I have found that this clay's fragile nature, after baking, was less than suitable for large scale artist dolls like mine. My first doll, Sister Mary, was sculpted of Super Sculpey.

When mixing different brands of polymer clay, a big consideration is pairing clays with like curing temperatures.

For instance, Fimo cures at 230 degrees Fahrenheit, Cernit at 265 degrees Fahrenheit, and Sculpey at 275 degrees Fahrenheit. Just do the math.

My criteria in choosing a suitable polymer clay is the overall look of the finished doll and the lasting durability of the cured clay.

ARMATURES

Simply stated, polymer clay doll modeling is a laminating process. What is meant by *laminating* is that sheets of clay, after conditioning, are placed over an armature, modeled, then baked or cured.

An *armature* is defined as a foundation, frame, or core skeleton used to support the modeled clay. Armature components vary depending upon the particular doll part and the scale or size of the overall doll. Head armatures are usually composed of a compacted core of aluminum foil. Aluminum foil, Romex cable, and wire are best suited for appendages of arms and legs. The completed armature with the added clay should be able to withstand baking temperatures of 265 degrees Fahrenheit for at least an hour without melting or imploding.

My comfort zone is sculpting dolls with a sturdy stature of around 28" to 30" tall. I find that this size enables me to sculpt realistic detail into facial features, explore elaborate hairstyles, and design interesting garment ensembles. This scale also best communicates my desired design statement. The armatures that I construct must be able to support a tall, weighty doll of approximately 6 to 8 pounds with a top-heavy head and still retain its structural integrity.

Many collectors in urban markets prefer smaller dolls, as do other doll enthusiasts who have limited living space. When creating dolls for sale, this is a consideration.

The head accounts for a sizable portion of the overall doll weight on my dolls, so efforts must be taken to keep its weight as low as possible. The goal is to enable the doll to stand balanced and erect without faltering. A core of tightly compacted aluminum foil in the head provides stability and conserves weight.

I have also experimented with styrofoam wrapped in foil at the center core, as an alternative to the solid foil core method. Styrofoam *(polystyrene)* can help shape the desired look while keeping the head armature light. Styrofoam, however, may be an unpredictable element when baked, since it conceiveably can have a melting point as low as 250 degrees Fahrenheit. *(Note that polymer clay cures at 265 degrees Fahrenheit.)* But, since the styrofoam is positioned deep inside the head armature and is baked for only one hour maximum at a time, problems from elevated heat levels may not occur.

This is an unknown. It is always best to pre-test styrofoam by baking a trial piece to determine its integrity. It is believed that some grades of styrofoam, i.e., European-made styrofoam, are more stable than other forms. It may have a higher melting point, but I have not adequately researched or tested this theory.

SCULPTING STANDS

Armatures for sculpting and for baking must be positioned or elevated on a stable frame or stand support for ease in working. Since I have never really found stands that are commercially available for this dedicated purpose, I scour thrift shops to find bric-a-brac that might do the trick. I have also had custom metal stands made.

For head armature stands, I have successfully used random things like lamp bases and microphone bases!

For arms and legs, I have modified napkin holders and the like to accommodate the task. Custom-made stands are, of course, the ideal.

For ease in sculpting, I use a commercial sculpting turntable that is intended for a multitude of sculpting purposes.

It is obviously not intended for oven-baking. Turntables can be found in art stores.

Armature components—yes, this means a trip to the hardware store / building supply store!

Sculpting stands for heads, etc. Do I see lamp bases and microphone bases here?

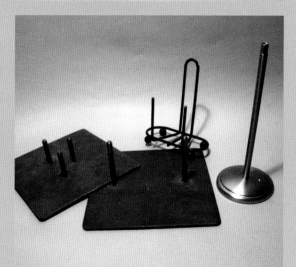

Various turntables.

Sculpting stands for appendages like arms and legs, including custom metal stands.

START AT THE BEGINNING—
HEAD CONSTRUCTION

There are numerous methods of engineering a doll's sculpted body parts depending upon important considerations of the doll's overall size, weight distributions, pose, and final apparel choices. The most popular and simplistic methods are explored here; although, one must customize the sculpt to suite the situation. Sculpting body parts always starts with the *head,* since it determines the doll's scale and it gives the doll a personality that may suggest the doll's final pose.

Flanged Head

The flanged head construction is the most simplistic and abbreviated of them all. It consists of a head and neck in one that is bordered with an edge flange. The flange edge, i.e., a projecting flat rim or collar edge, will ultimately be bound with bias fabric then sewn onto the torso. A channel or an indentation encircles the flange. It serves as a groove for wire, cord, and/or bias fabric which will then be secured by sewing the head to the fabric body. The flanged head must be seated firmly on the doll's shoulders, so as not to falter.

The sculpted flange edge, or lip, must slope a bit and not protrude as an obvious ridge. This will create a smooth transition between the clay neck and the torso shoulder. Note the angle or incline of the flange in the sketch. This is a subtlety that makes a big difference when assembling the doll.

Sister Mary, my very first OOAK polymer clay doll, successfully used this type of head design. The jewel neckline of her dress conceals the construction.

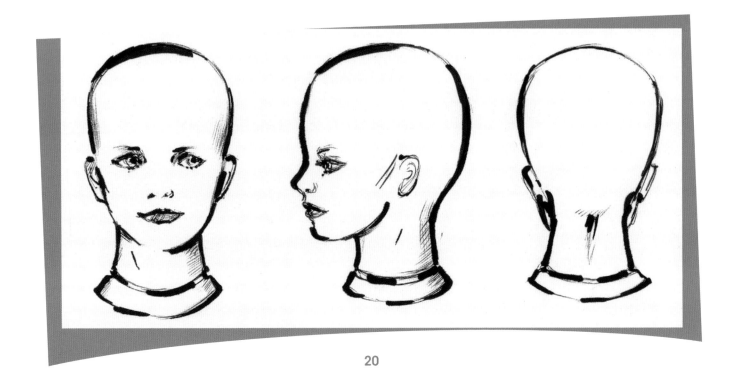

Socketed Head

The advantage of the socketed head construction enables the completed doll's head to be somewhat posed or cocked. The disadvantages are that a visible neck/head division will always be visible unless camouflaged by apparel or neck jewelry.

A challenge is that the upper torso may become weighty from the additional clay. During torso construction, weight issues will be addressed by counter-balancing the overall doll's weight by adding lower torso weights. (See the section on Soft Torso Construction.)

The socketed head can be used with a partial shoulder plate or a full breast cage. Note the curvature and angle of the back and how it differs from the front.

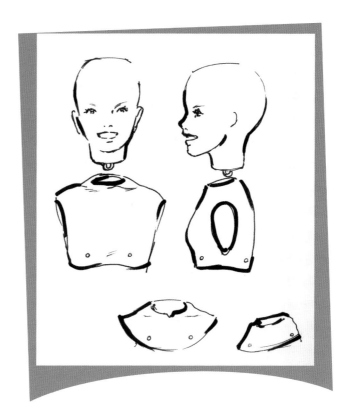

Head and Partial Shoulder: Construction

This engineering method works well for a variety of different sized dolls. A more relaxed and realistic look is attainable when the head is a part of the shoulder, since there is no obvious joint present at the neck. Apparel also works well with it, as long as there are no revealing plunging necklines.

Here is an example of the Head and Partial Shoulder method of construction. Keiko, shown here, ultimately wears a layered kimono ensemble, and very little of her neck is exposed when dressed. The head gently transitions into the upper chest and shows her sculpted clavicle, which always is a pretty look. This unit is anchored to the body with a strong cording, which is then concealed by a flesh-colored grosgrain ribbon bow.

When sculpting this method, it is best to avoid making sharp angles or squared off corners at the bottom of the shoulder plate. Sharp corners will become vulnerable to chipping and, more seriously, to cracking. A smooth graceful transition works best since it is a stronger engineering solution. It has more structural integrity.

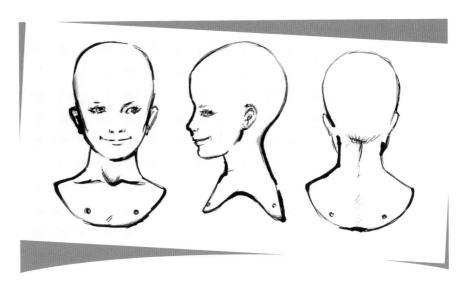

21

I particularly like sculpting this method, and you can re-use the aluminum foil shoulder armatures or bases in most cases.

I like reinforcing the inside of the shoulder plate with **Durham's Water Putty**. It hardens much like a plaster, and it gives an added strength to the cured clay. The plate will undergo some pressure when attached to the torso, so this added measure is very practical.

Head and Torso in One Unit

A full or partial body sculpt is recommended only for small dolls for simply practical reasons. Not only may the doll's weight become a problem, but the doll's overall sculpted mass may be too large for the curing oven, which is most often one's kitchen oven with its limited space capacity.

Also, sculpting in segments rather than in an entire body mass reduces the risk of minor problems becoming a problem to the entire doll. A serious crack that may arise in the cured one-unit piece may ruin the whole doll; whereas, if the doll were sculpted in segments, the flawed piece could easily be replaced without effecting the whole body.

Distribution of weight is an important consideration in constructing a doll. If the doll is too top-heavy, this increases the possibility of the doll toppling over, losing balance, and then becoming vulnerable to breaking.

Take care in utilizing this extended head and torso method.

HEAD ARMATURE

The subject doll being created here in the studio is the beloved storybook character *Pippi Longstocking*. Pippi's armature is made of firmly packed aluminum foil underneath the masking tape layer exterior shown here. (See Pippi on pages 48–49.)

Tightly condense a ball of aluminum foil, exposing the dull side out. Construct the ball in an approximate shape a little smaller than the desired finished head, making allowance for the clay layers to come.

Creating a loose ball will result in structural problems during sculpting and may cause the work to relax and depress unevenly in vulnerable areas that are not firm. A tightly compacted foil core makes an effective and stable head foundation.

Warning: The foil may "grin" through, or show through thin areas of clay and tend to shade it. The dull side of foil repels light, and is less likely to show through the clay layer than the shiny side, in my experience. This is not so much of a concern when it is covered with tape, but this is my practice.

Take precautions to add an ample layer of clay to avoid unwanted shading from the foil, if masking tape is not used. The clay layers may ultimately vary in depth from approximately ⅜" to ¾".

I cover the armature with masking tape, both to avoid fly-away foil ends and to prevent the foil from grinning through.

Two hollow indentations are made in the head armature that will house the doll's glass eyes. The glass eyes will remain in the head during baking. Anchor the eyes in the head by placing a dab of polymer clay in each socket, then position the eyes.

I prefer glass eyes over acrylic eyes, even though both can withstand the low fire required to cure the polymer clay. Acrylic eyes are known to possibly change color with time, probably from heat and exposure to strong daylight.

Here is the head armature ready for clay sculpting. The shoulder base armature that the head is resting on is constructed of foil and masking tape, like the head. It can be re-used time and time again

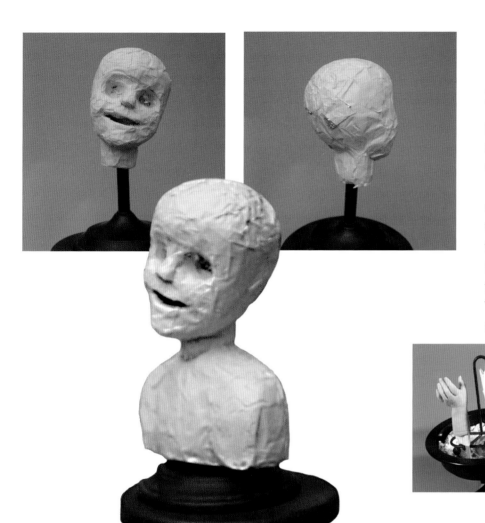

Arms

There are numerous methods of engineering a doll's sculpted body parts depending upon important considerations of the doll's overall size, weight distribution, pose, and final apparel choices. The armature and sculpt are customized to suit the needs of the situation.

My doll armatures for limbs contain a hefty 10 gauge insulated electrical cable, aka *Romex,* as main vertical supports with 16 gauge wires for fingers and toes. This skeleton is then wrapped with aluminum foil to create contour and form, prior to clay sculpting. Here again, it is best to layer the aluminum foil with the dull side out, then wrap the armature with masking tape, fully covering the foil underneath. The masking tape prevents a *"grin through,"* or appearance of dark streaking of the dark aluminum foil beneath the fired clay layer.

There may be variations on the length of the limbs, which primarily depend upon the pose and choice of garments.

In the case of a leg that stops under the knee, the fabric portion of the leg will include a pleated knee, enabling the doll to pose in a sitting or bending position. Most arms and legs are sculpted with a flange or collar rim construction method that facilitates attaching it to the soft fabric body.

Here is Pippi's abbreviated right arm after baking. The arm on your right shows the masking tape base which houses the cable and wires. The wires are inside the fingers to give them stability. Note how much smaller the armature proportion is compared to the finished arm.

Fingernail indentations and actual translucent clay fingernails are sculpted into the baked finished hand. Later they will be painted to look natural.

Pippi's final pose will show her arms raised and extended to hold up her pigtails. A decision was made to abbreviate the arm length

for future dolls.

Pippi's eyes will be placed in their socket indentations prior to sculpting with a small clay anchor. An ample opening was made to accommodate a future tongue and teeth.

A doll's eyes and mouth are thought of as being a doll's strongest attraction.

to this particular point, since her finished arm pose will show bent elbows. A longer length may have made bended arms awkward, and the added weight of longer arms would have been problematic as well. See her final Gallery photo for the pose.

The metal armature base holding the two arms is oddly a napkin holder with the two stylistic ball ends removed, but it serves well for this particular task (see photo on page 23).

Legs

Pippi's legs are surrounded by Romex 10 gauge electrical cable in this photo. Romex was used as a lengthwise core support for each leg, then wrapped with tightly packed aluminum foil for the armature. Masking tape is then wrapped around it. A portion of the Romex extends out beyond the leg as a base for attaching more wire. Note the flange construction used in the legs, also similar to the arm construction.

After curing at 265 degrees Fahrenheit for approximately fifty-five minutes and then cooling down, most of the foil and masking tape have been gently removed with long needle-nose pliers. The intention is to create a cavity in the legs down as far as is safely possible without causing damage to the sculpted clay leg walls. This is done after the cured legs are totally cooled, and not before.

The cavity in the legs is then filled to the top with a Water Putty by Durham. This solidifies and provides weight and anchors the Romex in place. Additional Romex will be added later to extend the leg wires. Eventually, the Romex will be threaded through a PVC tee fitting. This will be further discussed as we proceed to the body assemblage section. The legs are dried overnight.

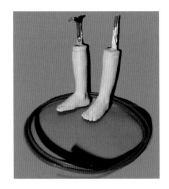

HEAD AND PARTIAL SHOULDER

Assembly

After the firing of Pippi's head/shoulder plate and arms and legs, the next step is to sand and refine the pieces using fine metal files and sandpaper from rough to fine grits in this order. The pieces will then be ready for attachment within the doll's body.

A compound called *Durham's Rock Hard Water Putty* is indispensable in the doll making process. Just add tepid or warm water and it activates and becomes like a durable plaster of Paris. It does not expand or contract once it has hardened and is super strong. It is used to fill the cavities of the doll's head and body parts to accommodate their attached hardware. This will ultimately add more weight to the doll parts, but this is a good thing.

Foil and masking tape are removed after firing and cooling to make room for Rock Hard in all sculpted body pieces. I use long-nose pliers and ever so gently remove as much of the foil and masking tape on the armatures as possible without doing damage.

The doll's **head** will then be filled with Rock Hard, and a screw eye will be sunken in place for later attachment to the shoulder plate. Note the direction of the screw eye. There is a reason for this.

The **shoulder plate** will be coated with Rock Hard on the under side to add to its strength and durability.

It undergoes some pressure during and after it is attached to the torso, so this is an extra precautionary measure.

The **arms** will ultimately be bent to pose. Fill the short arms with Rock Hard after placing armature skeleton beads inside. See photos of *posed arm preparation* for procedure.

The **legs** are stationary and will not be bent as are the arms, but they will still be filled with Rock Hard, and the Romex will be secured inside. The added weight will help ground the finished doll.

Durham's Rock Hard Water Putty is easily found in hardware stores and building supply stores. Drying time is minimal, but I prefer drying parts overnight to be sure.

POSED ARMS: PREPARATION
OF CURED ARMS

Pippi's arms will ultimately be bent and extended, so the use of the *beaded skeleton* is essential. I prefer to purchase the skeleton in running yards on a spool for convenience. Smaller segments can also be bought commercially.

Each arm contains a plastic bead skeleton, shown here alongside the special tool that both separates and joins the beads. The purpose of the beaded skeleton is that it will allow optional bending and posing of the arms.

The beaded skeleton reminds me of the old "pop beads," but the skeleton is much stronger, and a specialized tool is needed to connect and disconnect the beads. There's no fun here!

In my experience, I also add a 12 gauge wire, threading it through the beaded skeleton. It gives added firm support to the desired pose. The beaded skeleton cannot support the weight of the arms alone without it. The wire reinforces its strength and holds the pose in place.

The arms are already cured, sanded, and filled with hardened Durham's Water Putty. When cleaning out the foil and masking tape inside the arms, the finger wires were left, but the Romex was no longer needed and was pulled out. It was replaced by the beaded skeleton prior to being filled with water putty. The wire is inserted in the arms much later.

Note that with this particular type of arm assembly, which will be in a single running length of the beaded skeleton, the directions of the beads shows one arm bead up and one arm bead down. This will be more obvious when the soft body is put together and all becomes uniform. But, if using the beaded skeleton, observe that beads will be embedded in each arm in opposing directions, so that they can join in one unit when applied within the torso body. The opposing directions of the beads may not be clearly seen in this photo.

COST SHEETS
(AKA INFORMATION SHEETS)

One of the responsibilities of a fashion designer is to create a cost sheet for each apparel item designed. I've carried this good habit over into doll making. Treat doll making like a business by keeping detailed records. Here are some reasons why:

In the unlikely event that **repairs or replacement** doll parts are needed, the cost sheet lists polymer clay specifics (*brand of clay, clay color, dye lot, paint colors, etc.*). Repairs or replacements will occur seamlessly, knowing this information.

The cost sheet serves as a good reference for polymer **clay flesh colors** used. Some flesh colors are more favorable to conditioning and sculpting than others, and they may even cure differently. Note your preferences on the cost sheet for future use.

The exact **quantities** of clay used are noted, as well as soft body fabric yardage, etc. This makes it easy to order correct quantities for future doll projects. The price of clay is dear, and knowing exactly what is needed conserves money and avoids inventorying surplus clay.

Attaching **fabric swatches** to the cost sheet provides a visual reference for the torso body, apparel fabrics, etc.

Dolls are cataloged here in a dated **chronology.** This serves as a reference library or **inventory** of dolls completed.

The doll's size or **height** is noted. This measurement is asked for repeatedly in competitions and in any descriptions of the doll.

The **head size** or girth above the ears is noted for use in ordering wigs or hats.

A suggested size for the showcase or **display case** is noted on the cost sheet. Since artist dolls are fragile pieces of art, many doll collectors will want custom showcases.

A cost sheet sources **suppliers** and components like clay, wigs, lashes, showcases, etc., and makes it easy to reorder when necessary.

A **paint color** reference is helpful later on in determining the best paint colors to use on skin tones. Either color chips painted on the sheet or an attached color palette provides a good visual reference. Potato chip containers' 3" clear lids make great little palettes.

An idea of the time spent or the **lead time** on doll making production is helpful in calculating its proposed retail price.

The cost sheet lists prices of components, and aids in determining the doll's **basic cost** and proposed retail price, should this be the goal.

Cost sheets aid in bookkeeping and income tax **financial records**. Deductions for supplies will help the bottom line.

Let's not forget **photographs** of the doll. I photograph the naked doll as well as the finished doll, in order to log how it was assembled.

The original **concept boards** are a good future reference. I attach them and other pertinent information along with cost sheets.

Cost Sheet Template
Use the cost sheet as a **guide**. It's always best to customize it for your own personal use.

COST SHEET
ORIGINAL ARTIST DOLL

Doll's name _____ Date _____

Doll's height _____ Retail price _____

Description _____

	Supplier/Brand	Color/Lot #	Size	Usage	Unit cost / Extension
CLAY					
EYES					
EYELASHES					
WIG					
ARMATURE	Wire/cable				
	PVC parts				
	Aluminum foil				
	Weighted poly pellets				
	Other				

(place doll photo here)

SOFT TORSO	Fabric
	Body stuffing

APPAREL, TRIMS, FINDINGS

(place swatches here)

PROPS, DOLL STANDS

OTHER

IDEAL DISPLAY CASE SPECS height _____ width_____ depth_____

MISC. RATINGS (add up ratings and divide by 5 for an average score):

Lead time (days, weeks, months):_____
(time project took)

Supplies total cost: $_____

* Labor/Time rating: 1 *minimal time—under 1 month*   Average:_____
2 *approximately 6–8 weeks*
3 *moderate time—9–12 weeks*
4 *moderately intensive—4–6 months*
5 *highly labor intensive—Awesome!*

** Quality/Appeal evaluation: 1 *not so good*   Average:_____
2 *below average*
3 *average appeal*
4 *above average*
5 *best quality Good job!*

SUMMARY: Labor/Time rating _____   Cost extension _____
Quality/Appeal rating ____   Wholesale price _____
Average of the two _____   Retail price _____

* Labor/Time is based upon the length and complexity of the doll making process.
** Quality/Appeal is based upon Design theme, Sculpting/finishing, Painting,
Materials used, and Costuming factors.

Production, Part 2

CONDITIONING AND PREPARING CLAY

Conditioning clay is an essential part of preparing the clay for sculpting. If it is not conditioned properly, negative results will appear during firing—guaranteed. It starts with working the clay in the warmth of your hands, i.e., rolling, stretching, and compressing the clay, resulting in the clay becoming softer, more pliable, and less brittle.

Conditioning time will vary depending upon the brand of clay, color, age of the clay, and moisture or oil content of the clay. Conditioning time may also vary when blending more than one color together.

I find that a room temperature of 65 to 72 degrees Fahrenheit, with low humidity, is most ideal for conditioning and sculpting. Warmer temperatures may cause clay to become tacky and too soft for sculpting. Clay can actually start to droop with warm temperatures and too much handling. If this occurs, set it aside and return to it when the clay and the room temperature are more favorable. A cooler temperature clay can also be cautiously pre-warmed in a heating pad. I use this with care only when the clay is somewhat cold and brittle.

There are some softening agents available for polymer clay that will aid in conditioning. Fimo makes *"Mix-Quick,"* and Sculpey makes *"Sculpey Diluent,"* which is a liquid for softening. ProSculpt is inherently pliable, so nothing is needed here, but a stubborn Cernit can benefit with a couple of drops of mineral oil. Also, a small amount of a soft translucent clay can be blended with a resistant polymer clay to yield better results without altering color.

ProSculpt Smoothing Oil is another product that is great for prepping and refining sculpted parts prior to baking, but I have not used it as a softening agent and cannot remark about its success.

Some polymer clays can be too brittle and crumble due to their oil being over-leached over time, or their exposure to heat. Polymer clay hardens in temperatures of 250–275 degrees Fahrenheit. Also, if left in an unattended vehicle or in the sun, clay is vulnerable to baking or partially baking and cannot be revived once this happens.

Purchase clay from a reputable clay supplier who has a good clay turnover, and remember to store your polymer clay supply in a cool, dark place. Light can also take a toll on clay.

If a recently purchased clay appears crumbled and resistant to conditioning, return it, and shop for another supplier. Avoid having clay shipped during the warm summer months. While the clay is in transit, it may also conceivably spend a weekend in a warm warehouse. Order clay in the beginning of the week when weather is favorable, and avoid prolonged shipping time.

NEVERknead Press

The NEVERknead brand tool press is an ideal apparatus for conditioning polymer clay, and it's especially a lifesaver for arthritic hands.

It's also ideal for mixing clay colors. Conditioning clay by hand can be tedious and lengthy, and the NEVERknead press is a real time-saver. It exerts the equivalent of a half ton of pressure!

This cast iron and steel tool weighs almost 20 lbs, making it sturdy and up to the task. I bolted mine to my sculpting table, as you will see.

It was created for polymer clay artists by a polymer clay artist out of her frustration of tiresome clay conditioning. It has a lifetime warranty. No, this isn't an advertisement. It's just one of my favorite studio tools and my personal unsolicited testimonial.

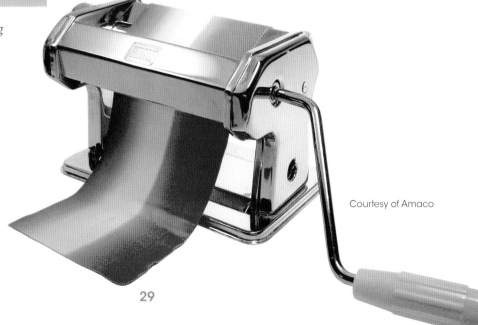

The NEVERknead press is invaluable for blending colors, as well as conditioning clay.
Courtesy of NEVERknead

Pasta Machine

A pasta machine dedicated to polymer clay conditioning is a basic must-have in the studio. There are many machines on the market that will do nicely—both manual and motorized. Some are dedicated to polymer clay only, and others are kitchen pasta making machines that have been repurposed to polymer clay use. I prefer a pasta machine that offers more layer width alternatives.

This pasta machine by Amaco, aka the *clay crafting machine*, will produce thin sheets of clay in nine alternative width settings ranging from .07 mm to 2.269 mm or a bit less than 3/32".

This type of machine both conditions clay, and blends colors together. Many clay layers will ultimately be positioned over the doll's armatures.

I have also bolted down this machine on my sculpting table. It works out well, since some torque or force occurs when turning the handle. Both the manual NEVERknead press and the Amaco crafting machine are life-savers in conditioning all types of polymer clay, and in forming uniform clay layers for sculpting. Here again is my unsolicited testimonial. They both are stars in my studio.

Courtesy of Amaco

SCULPTING TABLE

My sculpting table of choice is, of all things, a rolling bedside table, just like the ones used in hospitals.

I've had both the pasta machine and the NEVERknead press bolted to the table for convenience and stability.

The rolling table can be relocated to any room or even outdoors. You are now mobile, and you can follow the daylight, join the family, and catch up on your favorite TV shows. Think of it as a "pop-up" studio!

SCULPTING TOOLS

I use this silicone Catalyst brand wedge tool to smooth over sculpted clay plains. It is especially effective on doll faces, arms, and legs.

Wooden tools are wonderful for polymer clay sculpting. They leave no trace marks on the clay like metal tools, and are easy to use. The tool at the right of the group is flat on one side and convex on the other. It's point is great for getting into difficult crevices. It's my very favorite tool.

These polymer clay sculpting/shaper tools are used for modeling. The silicone ends or nibs are clean and adaptable to various sculpting needs. The silicone nibs come in many shapes and sizes and offer a variety of choices.

The only metal tools I use are a disc for cutting clay, an X-ACTO knife, and long sewing needles for piercing holes.

A metal semi-curved tool is used for fingernails and for extracting small quantities of clay.

AFRICAN HEAD ANATOMY

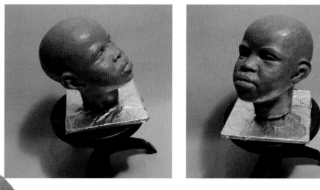

As an artist of all ethnic groups, I particularly enjoy creating black dolls. Here are some observations: When sculpting a classic black head and face, note the elongated facial planes of the head, the upward slanting forehead, and diagonal facial slope. The mouth structure may protrude beyond the nose which tends to be rather flat. The lips are full and the nose is wide. Other facial plains still have dimension due to fatty deposits.

Various shapes of noses appear to be tied to humans' adaptations to climate. The nose must properly heat and humidify the air that is breathed. In colder climates, it is advantageous to have a longer, narrower nose which will maximize the surface area and allow the air to be warmed before entering the lungs. Above, we see a shorter, wider nose, which is best suited to the warm, dry African climate. Nature is so wonderful that way.

One-of-a-kind doll making in this book focuses on polymer clay; however, I am displaying this non-polymer clay head as an example of an ethnic head for the sole purpose of design. This particular head is sculpted of *Roma Plastilina*, an oil and wax-based non-hardening modeling material that is permanently pliable. Here, it is used in a prototype model for an African porcelain doll head. Roma Plastilina can be re-used after the mold is made.

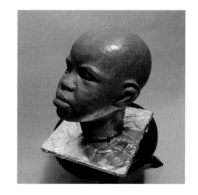

Here are other views of the facial architecture of this black head. The head is in unrefined clay.

31

SCULPTING

As I had mentioned previously, sculpting with polymer clay is a laminating process whereby multiple sheets of clay are placed over armatures or skeletons. The clay thickness will invariably differ on the same piece. For instance, the nose can reach ¾" to ⅞" thickness after adding clay. The cheeks can be ½" thick or so. Layers produced from the pasta machine will be laminated one over the other on the armature, then sculptured and manipulated. At this point, sculpting is both an adding and subtracting process. Additional clay is added for noses, ears, eyebrows, etc.

After curing or firing, the result will become more of a subtracting process during sanding and refining when the piece is smoothed.

Observe life's subtleties when undertaking sculpting. Unnoticed areas like the fat deposits under eyes and double creases in a smile make a difference between lifelike results and a bland amateur-sculpted face. Also, facial symmetry does not have to be exact. Manufactured widget dolls are always totally symmetrical and seemingly perfect, but in real life, faces are not necessarily geometrically correct.

The amazing dolls of Anne Mitrani are noticeably and some-times awkwardly asymmetrical. In her art dolls, one eye will appear substantially lower than the other, but the result is truly believable and realistic. It's fun to experiment with asymmetry, especially when the doll's head will be cocked to one side and facial tissue would ordinarily droop a bit on a real face. I did this with my doll *Little Apache.* This resulted in a facial expression that came across both as realistic and appealing to those who have remarked about her. (See Little Apache on pages 84–85.)

Hands and feet always seem to bewilder doll makers. Here again, it all starts with observing life. If necessary, work with a model and take photos for reference. Clip pictures of hands and feet from magazines, etc. Keep a good reference file if this is a weak point in your sculpting. Study proportions.

Shown here is an illustration of a simple eye. The eye is not a perfect symmetrical almond or elliptical shape in nature. Note that there is a slight angle or distortion in the eye. When translated into clay, this can be a subtle innovation to make a doll appear more realistic.

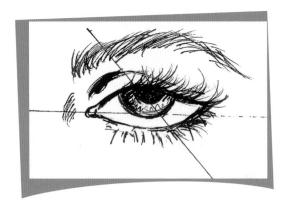

Head Sculpting

Pippi, our subject doll's lips, tongue, and mouth lining were sculpted with custom color-blended polymer clay in a color that is a bit deeper than her flesh color. Don't be afraid to mix different polymer clay brands for this purpose. A natural realistic look is desired for a contrasting color that is soft and age appropriate.

Blend clay in a lighter color, since the color will surely darken post-firing. Darker unfired clays will appear fine when raw, but will bake darker than you may desire. And, yes, it is best to pre-test.

Her teeth were sculpted in a translucent white Cernit polymer clay. Real teeth have a translucency and are not opaque. Crooked or distinctive teeth can definitely add personality and character to a doll. Remember, I don't make runway models!

All white clays are not the same, so it is best to test and pre-bake white clays for just the right realistic teeth color.

I have had the experience where teeth that were intended to be an optic white have sadly turned out slightly gray or yellow, enough to be noticeable. This is an important thing to control, and patch-ups with paint won't remedy the problem.

Avoid acrylic eyes. Use glass eyes only. My experience is that there is a good chance that acrylic eyes may change color in the baked and completed doll, especially with prolonged exposure to natural daylight. I've had dark brown acrylic eyes turn a bright royal blue like this! Thank goodness it was still a color somewhat found in nature! It could have been much worse.

Head Refining

Pippi's head and shoulder plate were baked separately in my kitchen oven, each for up to fifty minutes at 265 degrees Fahrenheit. Had there been any imperfections resulting in the baked head, I could have made the repairs and then re-fired her for fifteen minutes more.

Polymer clay is wonderful this way, corrections can be easily made through sanding, filing, or even adding clay into pits or depressed areas, then re-firing. The fired head is now ready for filing and sanding. Note the irregularity of the unrefined doll's skin in the photo. This needs to be corrected before proceeding.

This method of construction will enable Pippi's head to turn and pose. The four holes or perforations in the breast plate will enable the plate to be securely sewn onto her torso after the head is attached.

CURING POLYMER CLAY

Oh, the memory of mother's kitchen and the wonderful aroma of warm homemade bread, roast beef in the oven, and the seductive scent of apple pie baking that seemed to fill the whole house with such goodness. But wait! We're talking about *my kitchen* here, and this is not happening. In fact, there's only the heavy throat-grabbing pungent reek of toxic clay in the air! And, yes, this is what happens when mother is an artist.

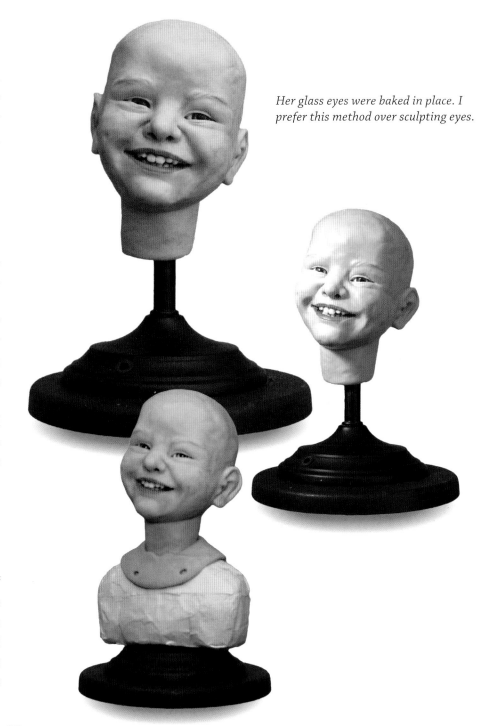

Her glass eyes were baked in place. I prefer this method over sculpting eyes.

My oven of choice for polymer clay curing or baking is the convection oven, since the heat is evenly circulated.

Conventional ovens are just fine too, but toaster ovens and microwaves should be avoided when curing polymer clay. Cernit's optimum baking temperature is 265 degrees Fahrenheit, so you can see how easily it can be baked in a home setting. The ideal is to have a dedicated oven for polymer clay for safety and health reasons, but that may not always be practical. I just clean my oven thoroughly after baking clay, and don't forget to open the windows.

Prior to baking, there's a wonderful product from ProSculpt that will aid in smoothing surfaces by brushing it on the clay parts. It is called *ProSculpt Smoothing Oil.* It is also useful in filling cracks or fissures that may have occurred during the curing process. Make a slurry of ProSculpt clay and the smoothing oil to mend flaws and smooth surface imperfections prior to firing, when the sculpted parts are in ProSculpt clay. Blend Cernit with the smoothing oil, in the event that Cernit is the sculpted medium that is being mended.

Sculpted parts should be as flat as possible when in the preheated oven. A head that is positioned vertically may find itself slightly tanned on its crown or on the tip of its nose. I lay heads flat, face side up, in a bed of cotton fiberfill in a baking pan that is lined with aluminum foil on the oven's center rack. Cotton fiberfill can be the same that is used for stuffing soft body torsos. The cotton fibers will not make impressions on the clay. Allow enough room within a baking pan, so the sculpted part will not touch or come in contact with the pan's perimeter or rim, or it will develop indentations.

The same can go for arms with vulnerable fingers, and legs. Laying them flat horizontally in a baking pan, in a bed of fiberfill works out better than positioning them vertically. Vertically, the fingers can warp. I've had this unfortunate experience.

After removing the cured doll parts from the oven, I allow them to cool normally. Handling the parts right away may possibly result in the doll's fingers snapping and other similar tragedies. Parts solidify during the resting process, plus they will be too hot to the handle comfortably.

If intentionally making repairs after baking or curing, raw clay can be added to the problematic areas, then re-fired. The ProSculpt Smoothing Oil can come in handy here for seamless repairs. A good rule of thumb is to allow fifteen minutes for every ¼" of clay layer to be re-fired. Leaving the parts in the oven longer or indefinitely may result in the particular clay part becoming a bit darker that the other doll parts. Use caution and keep your eyes open.

Surprise! Some colors of clay may change when baked. I experienced this when firing hand-sculpted Indian corn cobs for my Native American dolls. I used pre-formulated colors, not my custom-mixed colors, like yellows, greens, oranges, and browns for the corn. Sometimes, colors on the corn cob turned out a hideous neon chartreuse and most definitely not a color found in nature! It's always best to pre-test new colors you are unsure of.

PAINTING POLYMER CLAY

I'm a fan of *oil painting* my polymer clay dolls. I believe the results are more subtle and lifelike than results from water base paints. The drawback is that oil paint takes longer to dry, and paint colors will dry softer than when freshly applied. Acrylic paints are also a popular choice for painting cured polymer clay dolls.

Sennelier brand oil paints are the highest quality standard. The brand originated in France in the late nineteenth century, and were a favorite of the French impressionists. Today, they have around 145 colors available, and their oil paints are considered to be archival quality. The pigments are ground extra-fine and are *safflower oil-based.* Safflower-based paint is slow drying, but it will not yellow with age, as do linseed oil-based paints. Also, the pale oil results in lasting color intensity. The result is the highest possible tinting strength and a lustrous satin finish that has a buttery texture when applying.

Sennelier had developed oil pastels specifically for Picasso.

A similar safflower oil-based paint on the market is offered by Dick Blick Art Materials. The color offering is limited, but the cost is vastly lower than the French alternative.

Color work is best done in daylight when the light is clean and natural. And, color work is best done before 3:00 p.m. After that time, the light starts to change and true daylight becomes compromised. As a fashion designer, I did my color work on solid colors and textile prints coloring before 3:00 in the afternoon. This may be the standard in the design industry.

Painting Polymer Clay: Pippi

Pippi was really fun to paint with all those coppery freckles.

Her base color was in oil paint and after that had dried, her freckles were applied with acrylic paint.

Hopefully, I would have Ann Mitrani's approval here.

Pippi's paint colors are cataloged with a color palette, and colors are noted on the cost sheet.

Production, Part 3

SOFT BODY PATTERN

This is a custom pattern made for Pippi Longstocking, our subject doll. It will be cut in 16 oz woven wool felt color-matched to her skin tone. Notice the lengthwise grain indicated on the patterns. The woven wool felt fabric is a two-way fabric with no nap, meaning that there is no reason to cut all the pattern's pieces in only one direction.

Patterns can be placed up and down on the grain line. Cutting on the lengthwise grain ensures that the garment will drape properly. Cutting in the horizontal direction, or perpendicular to the grain line, may result in an undesirable final fit. There is more bounce or give horizontally, and this could result in distorting the final sewn torso and altering the desired drape.

The seams to be top-stitched CF *(center front)* and side seams *(on torso and on legs)*, are ⅝" and they will be top-stitched ¼". The direction of the inside seams on the front torso and front leg will be turned toward the CF then top-stitched. All other seams are ½". The heart is not seamed but sewn double and filled with a tiny amount of fiberfill.

The arm pattern has approximately 1¼" cap ease between the back and front notches. Note that a single notch always represents the front of a garment pattern, and a double notch is always for the back. There is an arm tuck that will be finished in a downward direction that gives a little shape and definition to the elbow area. The arm bottom border curvature allows for the elbow and a slightly bended arm. Note that the arm is called the sleeve at right.

This is a good basic pattern for the torso, and it can be adapted or modified for other dolls with different statures and purposes. I use a high-quality thread to both join pieces and to top-stitch the torso.

An upholstery quality self-color thread is strong and it has a nice sheen, too. (Self-color is defined as a color matching the fabric).

For hand-stitching, I use a thread used for wig making! It is strong and can be used singly. It won't have to be doubled. It won't snap when tension is applied and is extremely durable.

I like to use pinked (i.e., cut with pinking shears) strips to cover seams other than the double top-stitched seams. I use the strips on the shoulder, armhole, and thigh circumference seams.

The seams inside the arms and legs remain as is. The torso looks more finished when taking this extra measure.

The doll's heart can be used plain or signed with the artist's signature, doll's name, or date—your choice.

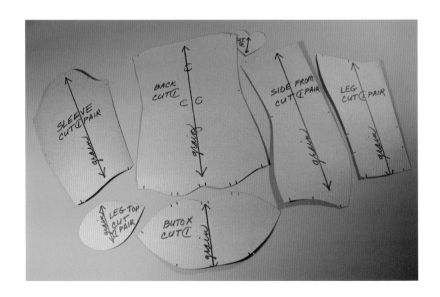

ARMATURES FOR SOFT TORSO BODY

PVC *(polyvinyl chloride)* is a tough synthetic polymer resin that is used in the plumbing and construction industries. For our purposes, PVC pipes make a stable and rigid internal vertical support or backbone for the doll's torso. Arm and leg connections are made and stabilized through fittings, or attachments to the pipe.

I prefer ¾" diameter *(inside measurement)* PVC *plumber's grade* pipe (not furniture grade) and the appropriate fittings for either end. Furniture grade is more expensive and unnecessary, since PVC is used internally and unseen. The strength and rigidity is there, and it accommodates small as well as larger dolls nicely.

And, yes, this means a trip to the hardware or building supply store!

When purchasing PVC avoid *threaded* fittings when possible, since they are troublesome and unnecessary for our purposes. You want *regular* fittings.

Supplies
(see photo on page 38)

pipe cutters

latex gloves

utility apron

sandpaper *(various grits)*

¾" diameter *(internal measurement)* PVC plumbers grade pipe fittings:
   saddle tee, regular tee, 3-way elbow side outlet, elbows, etc.

¾" PVC male adapter *(to use with a ³⁄₄" threaded saddle tee)* optional

couplings—couplings can add additional length through extension, in the
   event that you've cut the pipe too short!

Purple Primer *(I use Oatey brand, but there are other suitable brands as well)*

Medium Clear PVC Cement *(Oatey brand)*

PVC cleaner *(Oatey brand)* optional; used to clean soiled PVC pipe if new
   pipe is not available

Procedure

Use latex *(or substitute)* **gloves** for the glueing project to protect hands.

Measure the doll's soft fabric torso front to determine the finished desired size of the PVC pipe. Take into consideration the overall length of the pipe when the end fittings are in place, as well as the torso's seam allowance. Then **cut** desired length of ¾" diameter PVC pipe.

Lightly smooth the areas to be joined with **sandpaper** on either end of the pipe.

Swab **Purple Primer** on the PVC pipe outside end to be joined with the fitting, and the inside of the fitting. *Swabs are provided in both the primer and cement.* This will clean and prepare the joint for gluing. Primer dries immediately.

Then swab the outside of the pipe and the inside of the fitting with **Medium Clear PVC Cement.** Join together, then twist in place. This will help seal the connection. Then hold for about five seconds.

In the event that more length is needed to the finished pipe length, attach a **coupling** and apply in the above technique.

PVC ARMATURES

Supplies

3-way elbow side outlet (3 inlets) (good for some sitting dolls)

saddle tee socket fitting

plumber's grade PVC ¾" diameter pipe

regular tee (preferable not a threaded tee)

coupling—a transitionary adapter when adding length to the pipe; not shown
     in photo

latex gloves

PVC pipe cutters

Purple Primer & Medium Clear PVC Cement

not shown, but necessary: utility apron, sandpaper in various grits

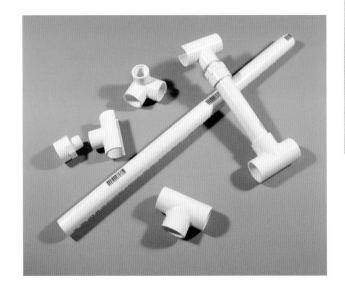

SOFT TORSO CONSTRUCTION

The body that no one sees is equally as important as the outside costume. I construct individual bodies for each of my artist dolls, depending upon their age, pose, and various factors.

As a fashion designer, I created lines of apparel and had a staff of professional pattern makers and sample makers or sewers construct the garments. When perfecting a garment that would go into production an average of around five samples of that garment would be made until the final sample was approved and released for production.

In home sewing, we do not have this luxury. Each item is an investment of expensive fabric and time, and each is basically an experiment. We give it our best effort and hope for the best.

Here are some tips in creating a soft body for your doll. I prefer a good quality fabric that tailors well and has body.

I use a 16 oz. wool felt that is color-matched to the doll's skin. It is a woven fabric, yet it has enough give. The body shell contains the PVC pipe armature and fittings, a sack with poly pellets for weight, and either cotton or poly fill. I prefer polyfill instead of a natural fiber since it will age better.

The pattern I designed for Pippi is age appropriate for her and holds her famous pose of holding and extending her braids.

Take pride in doing a job well.

I use a high-quality wool felt that is color-matched to the doll's skin. It holds its shape and tailors up beautifully. I top-stitch major seams by machine when easily accessible. A curved upholstery needle is handy for hand-sewing applications.

To prepare arms, place white glue in the flange indentation of the sculpted arm, then encase the sculpted arm inside its sleeve. Next wrap wire around the flange indentation with 8 or 10 gauge copper or other pliable wire. Conceal all this with a decorative felt strip that is then tacked on, i.e., stitched on by hand. Legs are attached similarly. It is wise to protect vulnerable sculpted hands and feet with either bubble paper or fabric before proceeding.

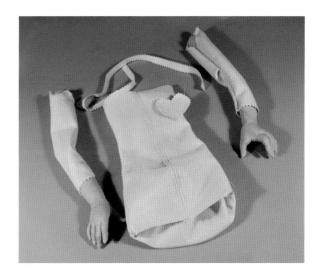

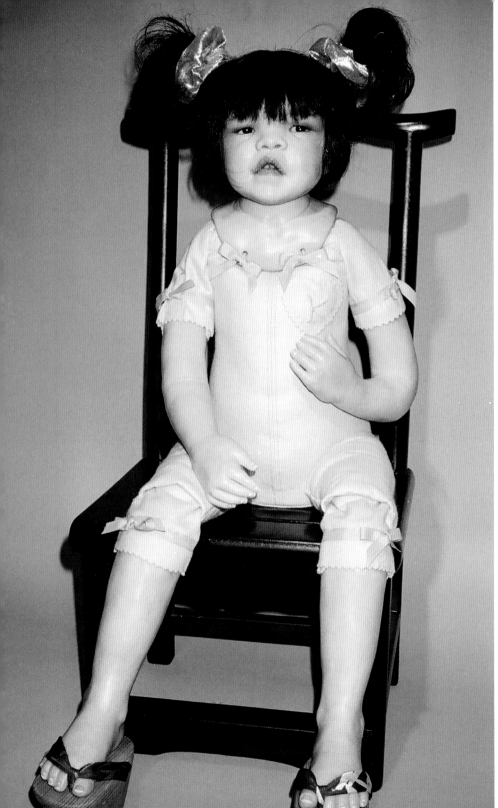

SOFT BODY ARMATURE

Let's get serious about the armature inside the doll's torso. This armature needs to support a sizable doll standing around 30" tall. It must be rigid and erect and ensure the doll's balance.

PVC pipe and its fittings or attachments make a wonderful and stable vertical support or backbone for the doll. Arms and legs are also stabilized through this armature.

The head is attached to the shoulder plate through the anchored screw eye in the head with stable and durable ⅝" elastic. Then, a 1" washer is placed under the screw eye with the elastic threaded through. The elastic is then whipped around the washer and tied. (See photo of head assembly on page 24.)

The legs are bound with more Romex wire arching from one leg to the other, then looping through the opening in the center PVC tee fitting. Another Romex wire that was added to the legs attaches to the vertical PVC backbone higher up. This helps fortify the doll's stature. Thinner wire wraps around the Romex, securing it. Lastly, 2" masking tape covers the wire and holds them in place.

When attaching the arms, the plastic beaded skeleton will be threaded into one continuous track with a 16 gauge wire inside of it. This will facilitate posing and bracing the doll's arms in place. The continuous arm skeleton will then be placed in the torso's PVC saddle fitting. I like to anchor it with masking tape.

Yes, finally there's a use for your old panty hose! Cut off one of the legs and fill it with poly pellets and tie it off. This apparatus will sit in the buttocks of the torso and will help equalize the doll's overall weight distribution. The poly pellets are easily found in craft stores.

Last, I fill the torso with polyfill—"cluster fiberfill" (Air Lite Manufacturing). I buy it in bulk, which is more economical than purchasing large quantities of small bags from craft stores.

Keiko is shown here in the buff! Her torso is a similar construction.

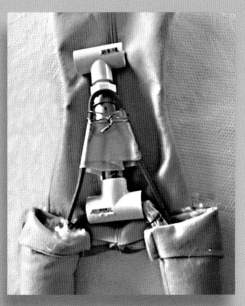
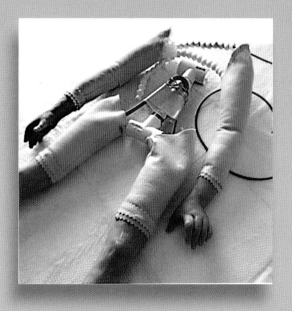

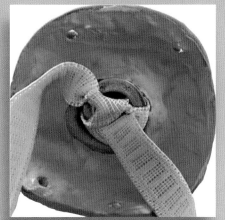

MARKETING

Whether doll making is a hobby or for profit, here are some considerations.

Create a **support system** in your doll making journey. Join a supportive association or guild of like-minded people. *The Professional Doll Makers Art Guild* (PDMAG) is a good example of a helpful and encouraging association of fellow doll makers. Jack Johnston, founder, is well known in the doll industry as both an experienced doll artist and an industry marketing authority.

The Guild is helpful in assisting with doll making questions and concerns. It can also assist in the marketing of your doll either as a one-of-a-kind or **licensing** it to industry corporations. Making one-of-a-kinds produces a limited income. A limited edition (LE) of your doll or multiples may be viable options to explore if you are thinking about a more consistent income or a career.

Prepare your doll for sale. Provide a signed **certificate of authenticity** and **care instructions** to your buyer. The certificates need not be elaborate, but they should look professional and contain the artist's signature. I also provide my buyers with care instructions for polymer clay dolls. There are many considerations like heat sensitivity, sun exposure, and even how an artist doll should be hand-carried. I limit this valuable information to one page.

Remember, always take **good photographs** of your work. Consult Pat Henry's book dedicated to doll photography, *FDQ: In Focus*, for invaluable tips on professional digital photography dedicated to dolls if you do your own photography.

When **pricing** your doll, research your direct competition and stay within a reasonable range. Underselling the competition is bad on so many levels and is ultimately bad for all.

There are a number of ways to market artist dolls today. Having a dedicated **website,** selling through a third party like an artist's website or a **gallery,** and showing at trade shows are just a few. Many artists have websites and they don't need to be extensive. Small websites that contain vital contact information and limited photos can be enough to spark a collector's imagination.

Artistic websites like Etsy and Amazon Handmade are also popular online sites that get a lot of traffic from eager buyers. Doll **trade shows** and conventions are also worth the effort. This is an opportunity to sell and to meet other artists and marketeers. I attended the NY Toy Fair one year, and I am still drawing upon my experiences there. I was able to sell two dolls, meet prime collectors, meet some of my favorite artists, and get exposure as a viable doll artist, myself.

Another avenue for one-of-a-kind doll artists to market their work is through **an agent.** The Dollery, owned by Kim Malone, is located in Massachusetts. It deals with artists and buyers worldwide. The Dollery represents a vast number of top artists and constantly updates the website and has periodic showings introducing new dolls.

Children of the Heart, owned by Susan Anderson, is another US agent dedicated to high-end artist dolls with an international clientele. Established doll agents like Kim Malone and Susan Anderson give collectors confidence when making expensive purchases.

Doll publications are a wonderful way to get exposure. Often the top doll magazines will consider unsolicited articles on dolls if you choose to write your own copy. Doll **competitions** are also a good way to become known. Competitions are publicized in the doll magazines, and it is worthwhile to subscribe to the top doll magazines.

Galleries are another avenue for exposure; however, their exposure may be more limited to local clientele. On the flip side, this may also be a good thing, if the area and clientele are affluent. Use caution in working with an **individual gallery.** They are usually a small business and may be more volatile to financial ups and downs. I am aware of a gallery that went out of business and learned that an artist lost some very labor intensive art pieces that had just vanished! A Native American friend of mine had to pursue a gallery owner in another state to get her money. Though these examples may be rare occurrences, be aware. Research the gallery, get references, and make contracts if this is something that really interests you. Always have good contracts or letters of agreement.

If your dolls are more **art** than they are dolls, consider art shows and art publications. Hiring a seasoned art agent may also work out well.

IN A GALLERY OR HOME SETTING

Display your artist doll with pride in a custom showcase. Whether it is in a gallery, in your home, or in a collector's home, a showcase is an excellent way to exhibit your doll artwork.

I encourage my collectors to purchase custom display cases tailored to the individual doll for a number of reasons. They enhance a living environment by highlighting a piece of fine art, the piece is away from curious hands, and the doll stays clean and dust free. Highlighting a special doll in this way may be a novel and brilliant solution as well as spotlighting a unique piece of art.

I note basic display case measurements on the cost sheet or information sheet, just in case it's needed.

For more information about custom doll display cases, please refer to the Appendix.

Here is original artist doll Frida Kahlo, *featured in the Metro Gallery after she won the Latination 5 Award in 2013.*

Keiko *displayed in a collector's home in Encino, California.*

First Aid
What Could Possibly Go Wrong, You Ask?

Yes, this is first aid for you. It is for mending mishaps and tragedies that occur in the handmade doll making process. But what could possibly go wrong, you ask? Well, let's start at the beginning.

DESIGN

I can't decide what to sculpt. This is an easy fix. Just go with the familiar. There are models all around you. Take a deep breath and imagine. Just decide what has heart for you. Even consider paying a model or an ordinary person for modeling and photographing their hands, their feet, their pose, etc. Norman Rockwell did this and the rest is history.

PURCHASING SUPPLIES

How can I avoid problems in choosing my supplies? For clay purchasing, go with an honest supplier who has a good clay turnover because you do not want aged dry clay. If it's on sale, be suspicious. If shipped, ship it overnight or two days so as to limit its exposure to potentially adverse elements and avoid weekend layovers.

For other components, craft stores like Michaels, Hobby Lobby, Aaron Brothers, and others, along with hardware and construction supply stores like Lowes and Home Depot, can all be good sources. When using an item for the first time, experiment with it if possible, before using it in your work. Keep careful records of what you use and how you use it to build up your own reference list of best materials for your work. Your cost sheet is a great place to keep notes.

Don't hesitate to check the Appendix for my personal favorite vendors and suppliers. They are not there by accident!

CONDITIONING

How do you condition clay by hand? Cut off a piece of clay that is manageable in your hands, squeeze it, roll it, smash it, twist it, and show it who's boss! When it's reasonably softer, put the clay in the pasta machine on the thickest setting and roll out a sheet. If the sheet is intact and not flaking around the edges, you've succeeded. If you don't have a pasta machine, use a rolling pin to roll out clay. Slightly moisten the pin and the tile surface used, to prevent the clay from sticking to the surfaces.

Don't forget to use the NEVERknead press (see the section on Conditioning and Preparing Clay) in addition to, or instead of, vigorous hand-conditioning.

How long should I condition clay? Soften the clay to the point that it is malleable. If you overdo it, it will become tacky and droopy. Aren't these two of the Seven Dwarfs?

Remember: Whatever you do, don't under-condition the clay. Problems will be compounded along the whole process. It will come back to bite you.

Tough clay that is resistant may need pre-warming. If the heat of your hand doesn't do it, place it in a heating pad, near a heat source like a lamp, and you can even sit on it! But, don't let clay get warmer than your body temperature. And, no microwave, please.

You can also add a softening agent—Fimo Mix-Quick, Sculpey

Diluent liquid, ProSculpt Softening Oil, mineral oil, and glycerine. Also, rub a little Vaseline on your hands before conditioning stubborn clay.

Why won't my clay condition? Possibly, it is already partially cured. Maybe it was exposed to excessive heat or ultraviolet light (in the warehouse, in the store, during shipping, in the trunk of your car, or at home sitting in a sunny place).

SCULPTING

Eyes

Which eyes should I choose? There are a few different options in glass eyes: *half round, full round, paperweight, blown glass eyes, and oval.* Note that the blown glass eyes, which are fabulous, have a delicate stem in the back that could snap off when setting them in the clay head. The choice is up to you. I like to have my dolls look off to one side, so round eyes work best for this. Half round or paperweight eyes are pretty much stationary, and they focus forward.

I also like eyes that have larger pupils.

Larger pupils give the impression of innocence and youth. But, it is difficult to find eyes with larger pupils. Most glass eyes have small beady pupils! Small pupils come across as suspicious and untrustworthy, I think.

What size eyes should I use? One baby doll artist has it down to a simple formula. She chooses a size of eyes to match the height or length in inches of her doll, i.e., for a 24" tall baby doll, she chooses size 24 for the eyes! This sounds too good, but nothing can be this simple, I say. For my 29" to 30" tall dolls, I choose a size around 20, 22, and maybe 24. But, I find that even specific eye sizes can vary by manufacturer.

I have even looked into prosthetic eyes, but under the best circumstances, they are exorbitantly expensive. I had heard that one of my favorite doll artists, Sissel Skille from Norway, uses prosthetic eyes in her charming lifelike toddler dolls.

Eye size depends greatly upon the age of the doll being sculpted. The eyeball is the only organ that does not change size in humans. This is why children appear to have large eyes.

There are wooden tools called "eye sizers" that are, basically, sticks with different sized balls on each end. The set contains six tools with twelve ball options in various sizes from small to large. They are useful in shaping the hollows in a sculpted head for the eyes, and may be somewhat useful in determining the eye size desired as well.

How do you attach eyelashes? With *Aleene's Original Tacky Glue*, a white glue. Use a toothpick, Q-tip, and eyelash tweezers to place.

Teeth

How do I make teeth? Teeth are wonderful. They really add personality to a doll. *Remember, that the eyes and the mouth are thought to be the main appeal of a doll.* I try to gauge the color of the teeth the same as the whites of the doll's eyes. They will look more natural this way. I find it best to pre-bake samples of different white clays to achieve the right clean color. Teeth are somewhat translucent, and not at all chalky or opaque. Go for translucent white clays and not solid opaque white. A good reference: I purchased a toddler teeth model set from a dental supply outlet that has been helpful when sculpting baby teeth. Check out the dental supply sources. They will have many choices of teeth models representing different subject ages.

Hands and Feet

How do I sculpt hands and feet? Here again, we put ourselves into our art. Those who have long lanky fingers will reproduce them in their dolls, no doubt. Consult photos and pictures in magazines for the best proportions that are also age and gender specific for hands and feet.

Ears

What about sculpting ears? Have you ever noticed how no two people have ears that look like? Ears are as individual and personal as fingerprints. My daughter happens to have the most beautiful ears I have ever seen, so she has been a great model for ears for my dolls. Richard Creager once offered a sculpted model of a man's ear available to sculptors, but I believe that it is no longer available. You can make your own ear model using special rubbery clays. I have not done that, but it might be worth casting my daughter's ear. Oh, and where did she just go?

CURING OR BAKING
(AKA OUT-OF-THE-OVEN HORROR STORIES)

What about curing or baking? Here is a good guide for baking the various clays discussed in this book: **Cernit,** 265 degrees Fahrenheit (30 minutes for every ¼" (thickness); **Fimo**, 230 degrees Fahrenheit (30 minutes for every ¼" thickness); **Sculpey,** 275 degrees Fahrenheit (15 minutes for every ¼" thickness); and **ProSculpt,** 275 degrees Fahrenheit (10 to 15 minutes for every ¼" thickness).

Why did a white half-moon appear in cured clay? It could have occurred with one of a few things—the clay, conditioning, sculpting, curing, or baking. Most likely, the *conditioning was incomplete*. Also, positioning the clay components lower and horizontal in the oven will help with consistent surface temperatures.

Why are there bubbles in the cured clay? Here again, it could be the clay, conditioning, sculpting, curing, or baking. Most likely, it may have occurred during baking. Always *pre-heat* the oven, and keep the clay pieces in the center rack in a horizontal position.

PAINTING

How do I paint eyebrows? This seems to be problematic to so many people. Start with the thought that each eye brow is different from the other, so it's not necessary to paint them exactly the same. I like to individually make brushstrokes that simulate hairs. Invest in a good brush that has a thin, long brush bristle about ¾". This brush is also great for painting lashes. Check in stores that sell artist paint supplies.

REPAIRS

When fingers snap off, what can you do? Re-sculpt the hand, patch with ProSculpt Smoothing Oil blended with clay, glue with 5-minute Z-Poxy or Apoxie Sculpt by Aves, or *call for help! Help is on the way! Consult with Yesterware Restorations* (see Appendix) if you opt to contract out the repair.

SHIPPING

How do I best ship my doll? When shipping your doll, always wrap the hands, feet, and vulnerable parts in small white towels. I use the white utility towels sold in bunches at most variety stores like Walmart. Also, wrap the doll and make a solid cocoon with bubble paper, and place it in a good solid cardboard box filled with styrofoam peanuts. Avoid lengthy shipping time, best you can. Avoid weekend layovers in the shipper's warehouse.

For other questions, consider checking my personal sources in the Appendix. They are not there by accident.

Also, don't forget about Youtube for answering a variety of questions. Just about anything you want to know is featured there with a tutorial.

Pippi Longstocking
Eleeasuk & Salmon
Morning Star
Frida Kahlo
Brooke II
Mother of Yellow Wolf
Hoshi
Savannah
Shaunna
Birthday Bonnie
Keiko
Kathleen
Daughter of Spotted Tail
Masako
Erin
Child of the River
Francisca
Budding Flower
Little Apache
Akiak
Ivory
Nina
Mahtzo
Addy, The Biloxi Miss
Little Holy Bear
Cheyenne
Sister Mary
Kicking Bear
Danny
Juneau & Baby Harp Seal
Chir'r'y
Golden Flower
Anika, Santa Lucia
Navajo Corn Maiden
Anne & Dolly
Warrior Mouse
Zola

Pippi is a beloved fictional character who gets
her name from her mismatched stockings.
As you see, her ensemble is as fun-loving
and mischievous as she is...raggedy patches, a
stocking scarf, and her unkempt braids. And,
of course, Mr. Nilsson, her pet monkey,
completes the look.

Pippi Longstocking

Sweden

In 1944, for her daughter Karin's tenth birthday, Swedish author Astrid Lindgren wrote a charming children's story about a fun-loving and wacky fictional character named Pippi Langstrump, translated as Pippi Longstocking.

Pippi's forceful personality, superhuman strength, and intelligence make her atypical for the time. Pippi's bright red unruly braids, oversized shoes, and quirky sense of style further define this amazing tomboy. Oh, and yes, Pippi has a companion pet monkey named Mr. Nilsson, as well as a horse.

Pippi has been enjoyed by children and adults alike for generations. November 14th is Astrid Lindgren's birthday, and on that day three annual literary Swedish awards are given in her name to support noteworthy children's authors. The monetary prize is quite substantial.

Pippi Longstocking is celebrated not only in the four books Lindgren published, but her story was retold in cartoons, movies, and a 1969 TV show. The books have been translated into sixty-four languages.

PHOTO: Lynn Cartwright

SIZE: 29"

EDITION: OOAK

CIRCA: 2016

COLLECTION: Storybook Artist Dolls

MEDIUM: ProSculpt

FINDINGS: glass eyes, human hair eyelashes, synthetic hair wig

ACCESSORIES: Mr. Nilsson, the monkey

Eleeasuk & Salmon

Inuit

Eleeasuk wears a traditional fur and leather parka that replicates one on permanent display in the University of Alaska Museum. The museum's parka was made from arctic ground squirrel, wolf and wolverine fur, and domestic calfskin.

The hand-made parka is an exquisite example of a highly sophisticated garment requiring complex tailoring that rivals any finely tailored French couturier garment.

The musk ox mittens and sweater are hand-knit by the artist. The mittens appropriately show an intarsia "good luck" fishing graphic motif. The musk ox is an animal indigenous to Alaska. Its undercoat fiber is called *qiviut* and it's believed to be eight times warmer than wool.

The doll's traditional tundra style boots are a combination of fur with sculpted soles to look like leather.

Historically, in the Inuit culture, each person has their own unique name. I, however, borrowed a name that I learned from a man I spoke with at the Fairbanks Museum. I felt that Eleeasuk's name captures the traditional musical sound of the Inuit language.

PHOTO: Will Gallie

SIZE: 19½" seated height; 18" salmon

EDITION: OOAK

CIRCA: 2000

COLLECTION: Born in America

MEDIUM: Cernit

FINDINGS: glass eyes, human hair eyelashes, human hair wig

ACCESSORIES: musk ox mittens; sculpted salmon

A fishy story…

    As a born-and-raised Minnesota girl, I often spent time on the lakes, and I was certain that I could sculpt a fish from memory, with little or no effort.

    Well, as it turned out, I found that I needed a reference for the fish's head, after all. A local restaurant graciously gave me a salmon's head, but it required me to work very quickly, since it rapidly become a little too gamey to comfortably endure! Then success at last!

Early on, I received a great and sincere compliment from my two dogs on this doll. Whenever they passed the room where I had Eleeasuk displayed, they did a double take. They probably wondered if now humans came in miniature!

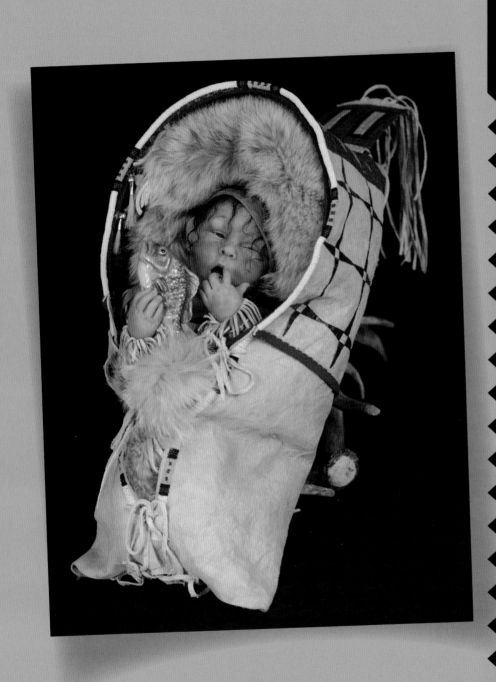

Morning Star's Lakota Sioux porcupine quillwork cradle bundle. The real beauty of this cradle bundle is the exceptional quillwork at the top, as shown in the photo below.

52

Morning Star

Lakota Sioux

The vibrant "morning star" motif was painstakingly quilled on this hide cradle bundle using berry stained porcupine quills. The quilled sun is bursting with rich and dynamic warm colors and is followed by complementary stars that gracefully cascade halfway down the cradle's sides. This enduring traditional design is reminiscent of the radiant morning sun and the promise of a beautiful new day.

The cradle's body is constructed of brain tanned deer hide and is lined with a brown classic calico print. Chris Ravenshead, the artist, studied quill artistry and technique under the elders of the Cheyenne River Reservation in South Dakota, where he later resided. His intention was to create a purist art piece that would reflect the spiritual and balanced Lakota way of life without contemporary reinterpretation.

Suspended from the cradle is a quilled turtle amulet, or charm, which traditionally holds baby's umbilical cord and has spiritual significance. A turtle amulet symbolizes a female child, whereas a salamander amulet symbolizes a male.

Baby whimsically holds a sculpted sunfish, which in Lakota culture is a fish often associated with children.

PHOTO: Will Gallie

SIZE: 31" lifesize in bundle

EDITION: OOAK

CIRCA: 2009

COLLECTION: Born in America

MEDIUM: ProSculpt, Cernit

FINDINGS: glass eyes, human hair eyelashes, mohair goat hair

ACCESSORIES: porcupine quill amulet, sculpted fish

53

Frida Kahlo

Mexico

Artist Frida Kahlo (1907–1954) was a Mexican self-portrait surrealist painter and a feminist icon. Her life's tragedies influenced and shaped her work dramatically and made her one of Mexico's greatest enduring artists.

At age six, she contracted polio and, while bedridden, found solace and amusement in painting. She began seriously painting at age eighteen, after being severely injured in a near fatal bus accident. Thirty subsequent operations ensued during her short lifetime. In spite of her misfortunes, Frida rose as a remarkable, talented, and striking individual who outsmarted her physical pain with her strength and resilience.

At age twenty-two, Frida married her greatest fan, artist Diego Riviera. He encouraged her art, and suggested she wear traditional native Mexican *Tehuana* clothing, which consisted of long, colorful skirts and exotic accessories. Their lifelong tumultuous relationship, though emotionally charged and riddled with infidelity, was mutually supportive of their art.

After the death of her beloved German father in 1941, Frida's physical and emotional health further declined. Later in her life, gangrene caused the amputation of her right leg. Pneumonia ultimately took her life at age forty-seven.

PHOTO: Lynn Cartwright
SIZE: 36" chair height
EDITION: OOAK
CIRCA: 2013
COLLECTION: Remarkable Women
MEDIUM: Cernit

FINDINGS: glass eyes, human hair eyelashes, custom human hair wig in Frida's unique style
ACCESSORIES: antique Mexican carved wood chair with velvet seat, sculpted parrot, period fabrics

54

Gangrene caused the tragic amputation of Frida's right leg toward the end of her short life.

It was my desire to portray Frida realistically, so this prosthesis was added to the doll. It replicates the one Frida had worn.

The exquisite hand-embroidered Oaxaca Tehuantepec Liensa *floral* fabric in Frida's skirt is vintage from Frida's era. It is edged in lace in the style of the region. Frida's unique braided hairstyle is custom made of human hair, then accented with signature giant silk flowers. She wears period jewelry and holds a colorful parrot, much like her real life counterpart would have done.

55

I always promise a story for each doll, and here we go...

A grandmother commissioned me to sculpt a portrait doll of her granddaughter, Brooke. After the doll was completed and delivered, an argument arose between the grandmother and the child's mother as to who would take possession of the doll!

In an effort to restore family harmony and peace, I was asked to make a second doll of the lovely child. Brooke II is the second of the two portrait dolls, but each of the one-of-a-kind dolls has her own unique expression and overall look.

And, there's more .

I not only had sculpted two portraitures of Brooke for the family, but was also asked to sculpt dolls of her cousin Marissa, and Brooke's mother, Dina, as well as her father.

A whole family of portrait dolls!

Brooke II, a second Heirloom Portraiture of a lovely real life child.

Brooke II

Heirloom Portraiture

Brooke II is wearing a coordinated woven silk and velvet sunflower motif ensemble purchased from Fred Segal in Santa Monica, CA. Fred Segal is an upscale boutique frequented by celebrities, movie stars and savvy Malibu pop culture. The store is known to carry rare and unique designer items. I think that her coordinated ensemble was an exceptionally smart choice.

Brooke holds a straw-filled toy antique puppy dog that appears to have been very well loved.

PHOTO: Will Gallie

SIZE: 34" tall

EDITION: OOAK

CIRCA: 2001

COLLECTION: Heirloom Portraitures, or Portrait Dolls

MEDIUM: Cernit

FINDINGS: glass eyes, human hair eyelashes, synthetic wig

ACCESSORIES: antique stuffed toy dog

At the time that I had sculpted Mother of Yellow Wolf, I was studying computer graphics in the San Fernando Valley, California. A fellow student, whom I believe had a crush on me, offered his "ponytail" to me for my dolls, after having his long hair cut. The hair was a wonderfully variegated gray color and proved quite striking and appropriate on Mother of Yellow Wolf.

Mother of Yellow Wolf

Wallowa Nez Perce

Mother of Yellow Wolf was a legendary real life Wallowa Nez Perce centenarian, also known as Swan Woman, who was first cousin to Chief Joseph.

Her son, Yellow Wolf, fought with distinction and bravery in the Nez Perce War of 1877, and participated in the tribes relocation to the Pacific Northwest.

Her fragrant smoky brain-tanned hide war-honor-style dress is embellished with beaded accents, including elements of horsehair, various teeth, and oxidized silver cone beads.

Mother wears native-made beaded moccasins, a sterling silver bracelet, and a beaded necklace.

PHOTO: Lynn Cartwright

SIZE: 14" seated height

EDITION: OOAK

CIRCA: 2000

COLLECTION: Born in America

MEDIUM: Cernit

FINDINGS: human hair wig

ACCESSORIES: Native American-made sterling silver jewelry, beads

Hoshi

Japanese

Hoshi wears the Gothic Lolita style, which is a sub-class of the Japanese-born Harajuku trend. She wears a black neoprene and velvet zip front jacket over a lace camisole and bouffant layered skirt. Her skyscraper platform shoes are partially covered with black velvet studded gators.

Harajuku is a fashion phenomena originating in the 1980s in the central hub area of Tokyo, one that has made Japan a global fashion leader. Rooted in Japanese pop culture, it is a whimsical and fun-loving clashing of East and West fashion.

Young locals dress in an informal mix of the unexpected from both worlds and socialize in their cutting-edge fashions at Tokyo's Harajuku train station, thus giving the trend its name. Styles are colorful and avant-garde, creative, feminine, geisha inspired, futuristic, and fantasy inspired. There are no rules here, except to be brilliant and have great fun doing it.

The street is the catwalk.

PHOTO: Jennifer Cartwright

SIZE: 31" tall

EDITION: OOAK

COLLECTION: One World- Harajuku

MEDIUM: Cernit

FINDINGS: glass eyes, custom human hair wig

ACCESSORIES: Gothic punk specialty hardware spikes and studs, Egyptian ancient Ankh cross, sterling silver rat buckle, hardware from Great Britain on a velvet handbag

60

Hoshi means "star" in Japanese. She models the Gothic Lolita Harajuku fashion trend.

The Naga tribe, consisting of around seventeen combined tribes, was a headhunting tribe and was known to preserve the heads of enemies as trophies. Savannah's beads are from this tribe.

Savannah

Africa

Savannah wears an exquisite Nigerian-woven caftan that enhances her unique individuality. Its asymmetrical styling adds artistic interest and novel balance to the garment.

Accessories like her native hand-crafted African Naga bead necklace, loom-beaded bracelets and hair piece, and giant brass Fulani earrings elevate her style to that of nobility.

Bold brass ankle bracelets over her bare dusty feet complete the image of this determined African princess.

Savannah holds a hand-painted African folk art doll.

Savannah's name was inspired by Africa's vast rolling grassland ecosystem called the savannah.

Characteristic widely spaced trees make this a rare and beautiful place. It spreads over many African countries and is home to exotic wildlife and vegetation. The savannah is the romantic focus of filmmakers, photographers, writers, and doll makers like me.

Note the dusty soles on her feet.

PHOTO: Will Gallie

SIZE: 19½" seated height

EDITION: OOAK

CIRCA: 2002

COLLECTION: One World

MEDIUM: Cernit

FINDINGS: glass eyes, human hair eyelashes, sheepskin wig

ACCESSORIES: Native folk art doll, Naga beads, and beaded African
   bracelets, brass ankle cuffs, giant Fulani earrings

Shaunna

Shaunna was inspired by the 2014 Sochi Winter Olympic Games, and one of America's favorite celebrity athletes of the event—Shaun White. She could easily be his little sister. Do you see the resemblance? They both have wonderful blazing red hair.

Shaunna wears an authentic native hand-knit Cowichan sweater and cap from the Coast Salish tribe of Vancouver Island. It is patterned in an intarsia knitting technique with mythological symbols and an American eagle on the sweater's center back. Other hand-knit and crocheted items are by the artist and her friend, Ginny.

Shaunna wears faux fur Ugg-style boots in her vintage wooden snow shoes.

PHOTO: Lynn Cartwright

SIZE: 31" tall

EDITION: OOAK

CIRCA: 2014

COLLECTION: Born in America

MEDIUM: Cernit

FINDINGS: glass eyes, human hair eyelashes, mohair goat hair wig

ACCESSORIES: sculpted snow ball, antique wooden snow shoes

Cowichan Native American iconic sweaters were considered to be a signature item for the 2010 Winter Olympic games. Instead of purchasing them from the Cowichan tribes of Vancouver Island, the Hudson Bay Company outsourced them to China for the event, which resulted in a lasting heated controversy.

Shaunna is inspired by the Olympic Games, but her Cowichan iconic sweater and cap are the real thing and were hand-knit by the marvelous and ingenious Coastal Cowichan Natives. Authenticity is my highest standard.

Shaunna started out with a totally different vision in mind. She was intended to be a tomboy with a sculpted frog emerging from her mouth! It's true. My friends who saw it hated it and urged me to lose the frog! Consequently, I added her teeth and tongue and went with a snowball theme. The winter Olympics were going on at the time, and this sporty inspiration seemed perfectly timely, even though snowshoeing is not an Olympic sport. This may very well be an example of art by accident!

Happy first birthday to baby with her papier mâché bunny.

Birthday Bonnie

One Year Old

Bonnie is a vision in pale pink for her very first birthday celebration. She wears a froth of a pink party dress with an embroidered bodice, and a whimsical child's knit cap with pixie-like ears.

A beautifully appliquéd first birthday cake is showcased on the dress bodice. Excitement is in the air, and Bonnie's bright eyes tell it all. Don't you agree?

Birthday Bonnie is my first attempt to make a pretty doll! I don't consider my dolls to necessarily be pretty, since I strive more for believable realism. To me, her beauty and appeal is in her bright expressive electric eyes.

PHOTO: Lynn Cartwright

SIZE: 17" seated height

EDITION: OOAK

CIRCA: 2007

COLLECTION: American Heartland

MEDIUM: ProSculpt

FINDINGS: glass eyes, human hair eyelashes, synthetic hair

ACCESSORIES: papier mâché bunny party favor

Keiko

Japan

Comfortably seated on a silk cushion on an Asian high-back rosewood chair, Keiko holds a very rare antique composition Enigma doll that still has a working voice box.

The luxurious red silk kimono fabric was purchased on one of my trips to Asia.

Keiko's custom hand-crafted wooden platform shoes with silk straps replicate the Japanese geisha's *getas*.

PHOTO: Will Gallie

SIZE: 28" tall seated in chair

EDITION: OOAK

CIRCA: 2002

COLLECTION: One World

MEDIUM: Cernit

FINDINGS: glass eyes, human hair eyelashes, human hair

ACCESSORIES: rice composition antique Enigma doll

Kathleen

Ireland

I find myself constantly collecting interesting items from auctions, antique stores, estate sales, etc. I have amassed a specialized treasury of doll clothes, props, and miscellaneous inspirational items. I carefully and lovingly store them for the right opportunity. My daughter calls me the organized hoarder, which is a title that I am not sure is a compliment or a put down! In any respect, yes, I do care for them in an organized way.

The antique milking stool and hand-knit Irish fisherman's sweater were great finds that I had kept safe for some time. With the creation of Kathleen, this was the right moment to resurrect them. The small three-legged antique milking stool has a marvelous patina from age.

The hand-knit sweater was in new, unused condition and still had the original hang tag attached by the artist. The sweater and graphics on the tag appeared to have been from the 1940s. The knitter was from Loch Garman, Ireland, and she had personally signed the hang tag. The yarn is 100% Irish Bainin wool, and the handcrafted buttons were made of Irish Laburnum wood.

PHOTO: Jennifer Cartwright

SIZE: 27" seated height on milking stool

EDITION: OOAK

CIRCA: 2009

COLLECTION: One World

MEDIUM: Cernit

FINDINGS: glass eyes, human hair eyelashes, mohair goat hair wig

ACCESSORIES: three legged milking stool, faux mountain heather

The Irish lassie seated on an old three-legged milking stool amongst the mountain heather.

And, a personal doll story…

Kathleen was a commissioned artist doll. A loyal doll collector had previously purchased a Norwegian artist doll from me, as well as a Swedish artist doll. Her goal was to collect dolls that represented her own ethnic heritage, and there was a need for an Irish doll.

The day I delivered Kathleen to my collector, she was not available, so I set the doll up in the designated spot in her living room. My display case maker had preceded me there and had already delivered the doll's custom showcase. I assembled Kathleen on her milking stool and placed her inside her showcase. I then left.

Hours later, I called my collector to learn her reaction to her new doll. She told me that when she first saw Kathleen, she cried. She said that it was because she was so beautiful! I live for these moments. Compliments don't get better than this.

Daughter of Spotted Tail

Brule Lakota

Daughter of Spotted Tail wears a remarkably ornate embellished deer hide dress. Besides the detailed beadwork, there is a profusion of more than 200 sculpted elk's ivory milk teeth on the yoke front and back.

The lifelike teeth were individually sculpted by the artist, then painstakingly oil painted to simulate teeth with aged tartar and dried blood. There are only two upper ivory milk teeth to each animal. This rarity makes them a symbol of great wealth to the tribe.

Yes, elks teeth historically signified wealth and prosperity, but in the late nineteenth century, elk became scarce and tribes could no longer hunt freely. Imitation teeth were then created from carved bone for ceremonial garments' embellishment.

This elaborate hide dress is designed in the Southern Plains style with a bold border embellishment laden with beaded detailing and tin cone beads that jingle with the wearer's movement. The traditional cut leather fringe on the border of her hem is a popular and practical feature, since it facilitates the drying process of a garment that may have gotten wet.

Unseen, under the dress, are luxurious fur leggings. The sleeves are also lined with soft fur. The dress is synched at the waist with a sterling silver native-made conch belt. Daughter of Spotted Tail wears stunning fully beaded Shoshone ceremonial moccasins.

And here is her story…

Daughter of Spotted Tail's name is Ah-ho-appa which means Fallen Leaf in Brule Lakota. She was Chief Spotted Tail's very favorite daughter.

She came to fancy a white soldier at Fort Laramie, and reportedly followed him about, dressed in her best enticing attire to allure him.

Eventually, her father found out and forbade her from seeing him. Legend has it that around 1875, she consequently died of a broken heart.

PHOTO: Will Gallie

SIZE: 14½" seated height

EDITION: OOAK

CIRCA: uncertain

COLLECTION: Born in America

MEDIUM: Cernit

FINDINGS: glass eyes, human hair eyelashes, human hair wig

ACCESSORIES: Native American-made sterling silver conch belt, Shoshone
fully beaded ceremonial moccasins

The fully beaded ceremonial moccasins she wears are beaded on the bottom soles. They are ironically also traditionally used as burial moccasins.

Masako

Japan

Masako wears a stylized Japanese kimono over a traditional Scottish plaid skirt. The Asian knot on the kimono nicely unites these two contrasting statements. Underneath is a rugby striped shell in sea tones that color coordinates with her shaggy faux fur Ugg-style high top boots.

The plaid Asian knot was a bit of a puzzle to construct, and if it hadn't been for my good friend Ginny's ingenuity in solving puzzles, it may not have looked this good!

Masako depicts the popular Kawaii style in Japanese Harajuku fashion (see page 60). Kawaii is a sub-trend of Harajuku in which the wearer looks like a young child or baby. Hair is often worn in ponytails, and clothing is youthful and colorful.

PHOTO: Jennifer Cartwright
SIZE: 30" tall
EDITION: OOAK or ProSculpt
CIRCA: 2012
COLLECTION: One World- Harajuku Kawaii
MEDIUM: Cernit
FINDINGS: glass eyes, human hair eyelashes, custom human hair wig
ACCESSORIES: beaded minodiere handbag

Masako's name means "proper child."

The Harajuku Kawaii concept is a whimsical blending of East and West. Here, Masako gives the popular pop culture hand-symbol as her sign of approval.

Erin

Heirloom Portraiture

Erin wears a holiday-inspired knit ensemble composed of a hand-knit sweater with a Santa Claus intarsia motif, coordinating graphic mittens, and a fashionable red beret topped with a perky snowball pom-pom.

Her tiered soft leather skirt conceals red tights, and she wears black-and-white retro saddle shoes not shown in these photos.

PHOTO: Will Gallie

SIZE: 19½" seated height

EDITION: OOAK

CIRCA: 2001

COLLECTION: Heirloom Portraitures, or Portrait Dolls

MEDIUM: Cernit

FINDINGS: glass eyes, human hair eyelashes, synthetic wig

ACCESSORIES: hand-knit beret and coordinating mittens

Erin is a portrait doll of a lovely and delicate child who had
health problems early in life. Her great delight was
experiencing the magic of snow at Christmas.
Erin kneels in the snow as she celebrates the season.

Child of the River

Salish Northwest Coast

Baskets, like this authentic Salish basket, were once used to transport goods and babies across the Columbia River. Here, baby is ready for the journey, nestled in warm snug beaver fur.

Baby's smokey brain-tanned hide tunic is accented with a fringe border, beads, and sculpted elk's milk teeth adornment. Fur leggings and Northwest Coast beaded moccasins complete the attire. The sterling silver and turquoise bracelet is also native-made.

Baby whimsically holds a squaw fish, as if it had flown over the river basket and Baby miraculously caught it mid-air.

PHOTO: Lynn Cartwright

SIZE: lifesize in cradle board

EDITION: OOAK

CIRCA: 2004

COLLECTION: Born in America

MEDIUM: Cernit

FINDINGS: glass eyes, human hair eyelashes, real hair

ACCESSORIES: sculpted fish, beaver fur

Baby catches a fish mid-air over the river.

79

Francisca

Mexico

Francisca wears a fiesta of vibrant colors in her ensemble of a vibrant cotton tiered striped skirt and embroidered blouson with matching hair ornaments.

Her beautifully embroidered blouse was actually repurposed from a vintage cross-stitch linen tablecloth.

Leather *huaraches* sandals perfectly accessorize her image, as she holds a classic leather folk art doll from Mexico.

This happy Mexican *chica*, or young girl, is comfortably seated in a vintage decorative painted wood-and-straw Mexican child's chair.

PHOTO: Will Gallie

SIZE: approximately 26" seated in chair

EDITION: OOAK

CIRCA: 2000

COLLECTION: Born in America

MEDIUM: Cernit

FINDINGS: human hair eyelashes, human hair wig

ACCESSORIES: vintage Mexican folk art doll, Mexican hand-painted decorative chair

Budding Flower

Navajo

Budding Flower looks comfy bundled in fur and this vibrant Chief Joseph commemorative wool blanket by Pendleton Mills.

The authentic Navajo bent cedar wood cradle board is native-made, as are the dream catcher and the turquoise and silver jewelry pieces.

The exquisitely beaded Sioux moccasins are also authentic native-made objects of art.

I first saw this electric hot pink blanket presented in this Navajo cradle at auction, and was truly dazzled by it. I easily imagined a cradled baby nestled inside the vibrant blanket.

PHOTO: Lynn Cartwright

SIZE: 32" lifesize cradle board

EDITION: OOAK

CIRCA: 2014

COLLECTION: Born in America

MEDIUM: Cernit

FINDINGS: human hair eyelashes, fur wig

ACCESSORIES: native-made turquoise and sterling silver jewelry, Sioux beaded moccasins and dream catcher

Little Apache

Apache

Little Apache wears a full length deer hide dress adorned with more than 200 *tinklers* or tin cone beads. The cones tinkle and resonate, providing soft music with body movement.

The dress's border fringe has both a decorative and practical application. The fringe, made up of hide strips, facilitates drying and repels water when the garment is wet.

Her sterling silver jewelry is accented with coral stones that match the coral colored beads in her dress.

Contrasting violet colored geometric beads accent her native-made hide moccasins.

Little Apache was inspired by a painting of the same name by notable western artist Ray Swanson. Ray was especially adept at painting charming Native American children with endearing personalities. And now, Little Apache takes on the life of a doll as a respectful tribute to this fine western artist.

PHOTO: Jennifer Cartwright
SIZE: 25½" tall
EDITION: OOAK
CIRCA: 2009
COLLECTION: Born in America
MEDIUM: Cernit
FINDINGS: glass eyes, human hair eyelashes, human hair custom wig
ACCESSORIES: sterling silver earrings, bracelet

Little Apache was inspired by a Ray Swanson painting of the same name. Courtesy of Beverly Swanson

Akiak

Yupik Eskimo

Akiak holds a precious antique seal skin native-made folk art doll that was purchased from a private Native American art collection. This unique folk art doll is highly prized and is considered to be museum quality.

PHOTO: Jennifer Cartwright

SIZE: 32" tall

EDITION: OOAK

CIRCA: 2009

COLLECTION: Born in America

MEDIUM: ProSculpt

FINDINGS: glass eyes, human hair eyelashes, human hair wig

ACCESSORIES: museum quality antique folk art doll, musk ox hand-knit mittens

This traditional fur-layered tundra dress is a popular choice with native Yupik girls.

Akiak's tundra dress has a sweeping border with a geometric graphic motif in the classic Yupik style. The exquisite red colored cross fox fur frames her face and dramatically accents the borders of her native hide dress. Fur leggings are layered under the dress, but are not seen in the photo.

The wonderfully soft mittens are hand-knit of yarn from Alaska's indigenous musk ox. Both the geometric patterned mittens and solid color wool sweater are hand-knit by the artist.

Akiak's tall tundra boots are partially sculpted to simulate leather with fur accent piecing and leather laces. This style of boot is practical and warm in the frozen arctic climate.

Ivory

African Elephant Activist

Ivory has a profusion of more than 200 hand-crafted multicolor African trade beads adorning her artfully braided hair.

Her vibrant woven cotton print skirt paired with her black knit crop top are peppered with charming gold metal elephant charms in varying sizes. Tiny buttons ironically show the backs of elephants on the blouse back closure.

Ivory's skyscraper sandals stand firmly on two ceramic elephants, reinforcing this doll's bold statement.

PHOTO: Lynn Cartwright

SIZE: 30" tall

EDITION: OOAK

CIRCA: 2014

COLLECTION: Dolls to the Rescue: Saving Endangered Wildlife

MEDIUM: Cernit

FINDINGS: glass eyes, human hair eyelashes, synthetic braided hair

ACCESSORIES: gold-colored elephant charms, ceramic elephant shoes

This female elephant activist doll is the first doll in the collection Dolls to the Rescue: Saving Endangered Wildlife.

There are a total of twenty-two gold metal elephant charms in varying styles and sizes on Ivory's entire ensemble, including the two on her skyscraper shoes. Each of the twenty-two charms sadly represents 1,000 elephants that were poached in 2013 for their ivory, then left to die. Ivory, activist doll, is the debut doll in this significant collection, and twenty-five percent of her sale goes to a pertinent charity that is dedicated to assisting in stopping the despicable act of elephant poaching.

Every doll has a story…

Ivory's story is a sad one, but it is gratifying knowing that my doll making talents can go toward raising funds and awareness of the precious and endangered African elephants.

Nina's classic bunad jumper and apron were originally purchased from the Norwegian Seamen's Church in San Pedro, California, for my daughter, Jennifer.

The church was founded in the 1950s and has offered countless Swedes and Norwegians a welcoming place when they are far from their homeland. Today, the Lutheran church has been known to get visits from the crew members of the more than 160 Norwegian ships that port in San Pedro each year. It is a popular place to visit among Scandinavians all over California.

Here the national Norwegian costume is modeled by my daughter, Jennifer (whom I consider to be my best doll). She is also one of my talented doll photographers.

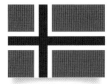

Nina

Norway

Nina's Norwegian national costume is known as a *bunad*. In modern times, it is a fairy-tale-like outfit worn for special occasions like festivals, weddings, ceremonies, etc. Traditionally, it is given to a child upon their confirmation.

The ensemble includes a red wool felt laced front waistcoat accented with wool trim, black dirndl skirt edged to match the top, and a white cotton lace apron over a white blouse or top.

PHOTO: Lynn Cartwright

SIZE: 27"

EDITION: OOAK

CIRCA: 2004

COLLECTION: One World

MEDIUM: Cernit

FINDINGS: glass eyes, human hair wig and eyelashes

ACCESSORIES: sculpted candle

91

Mahtzo

Apache

Mahtzo is nestled in billows of luxurious raccoon fur. Both the cradle board and the hanging burden basket are native Apache hand-crafted.

White Mountain Apache burden baskets are made from local grasses, willow, or yucca root. Since the Apache were once nomadic hunters and gatherers, the baskets served many purposes like carrying firewood, berries, roots, etc. The traditional tassels suspended from the baskets were edged in tin cone beads that jingled and warned off curious snakes while gathering.

Mahtzo's spiked hair is accessorized with a beaded headband to match his native-made turquoise jewelry.

PHOTO: Will Gallie

SIZE: 19" tall

EDITION: OOAK

CIRCA: 2002

COLLECTION: Born in America

MEDIUM: ProSculpt/mixed polymer clay

FINDINGS: glass eyes, human hair eyelashes, synthetic hair

ACCESSORIES: authentic Apache cradle board, Apache burden basket

Background image courtesy of Cowan's Auctions, Inc.

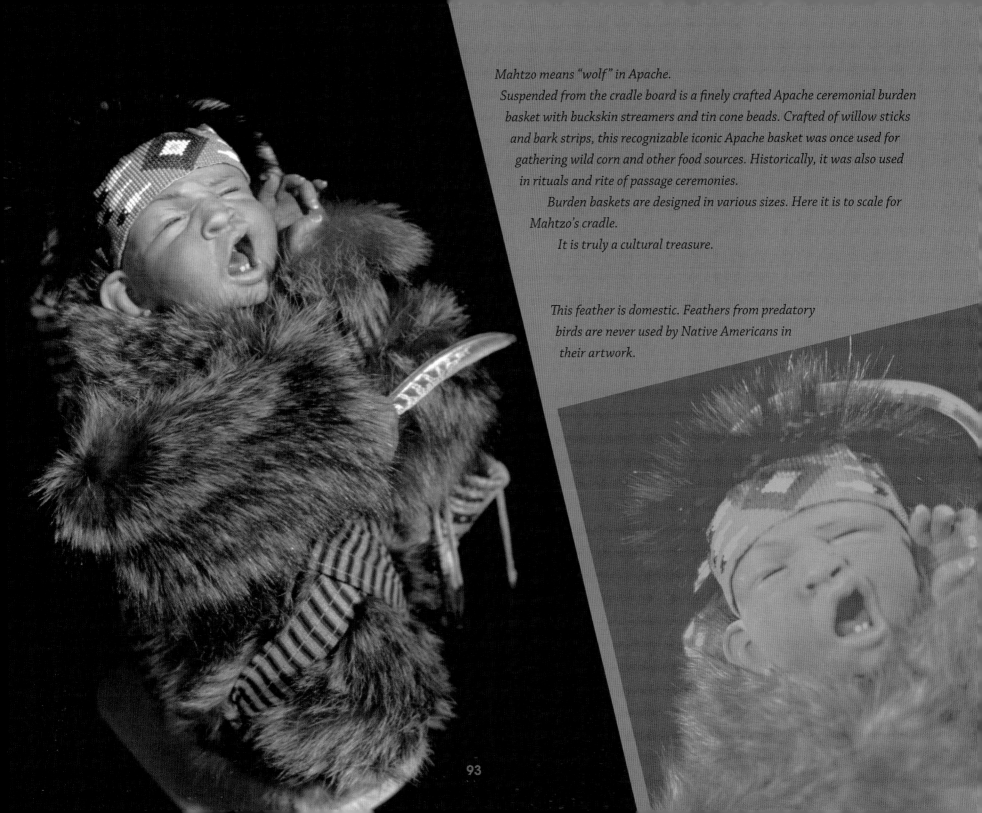

Mahtzo means "wolf" in Apache.

Suspended from the cradle board is a finely crafted Apache ceremonial burden basket with buckskin streamers and tin cone beads. Crafted of willow sticks and bark strips, this recognizable iconic Apache basket was once used for gathering wild corn and other food sources. Historically, it was also used in rituals and rite of passage ceremonies.

Burden baskets are designed in various sizes. Here it is to scale for Mahtzo's cradle.

It is truly a cultural treasure.

This feather is domestic. Feathers from predatory birds are never used by Native Americans in their artwork.

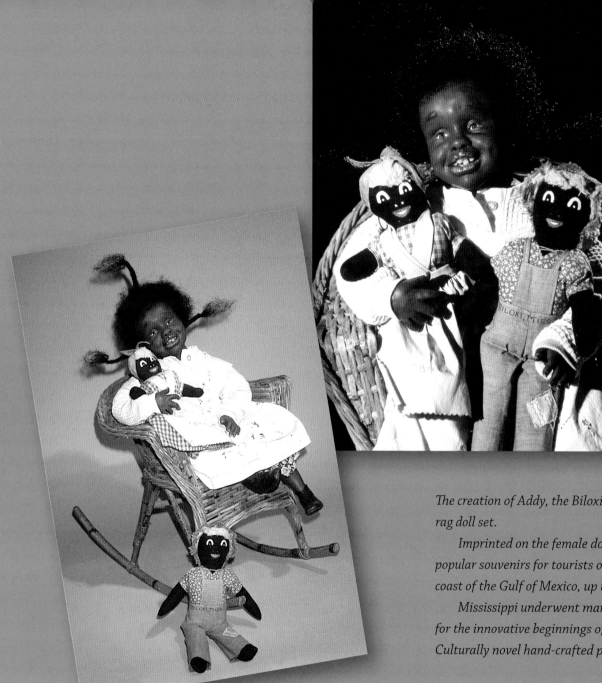

The creation of Addy, the Biloxi Miss, was obviously sparked by the companion vintage rag doll set.

Imprinted on the female doll's apron are the graphics "Biloxi Miss." The dolls were popular souvenirs for tourists of Biloxi, Mississippi, and were sold in shops along the coast of the Gulf of Mexico, up until the 1970s.

Mississippi underwent many cultural changes during the doll's era. It was a center for the innovative beginnings of gospel music, jazz, the blues, and rock and roll. Culturally novel hand-crafted products like the twin cloth dolls also were popularized.

Addy with souvenir dolls.

Addy

The Biloxi Miss

Addy has a zany human hair wig with impish braids that seem to fly freely in the air, as she rocks in her miniature wicker rocker.

She wears a retro-inspired embroidered country pinafore over a floral Liberty print skirt. Black hightop hand-sculpted shoes peek from underneath.

Addy's attire is meant to typify garments of the same era as her historic twin folk art dolls, which is around the 1950s.

She is one of my very first OOAK artist dolls, and her scale is much smaller than later dolls.

PHOTO: Lynn Cartwright

SIZE: approximately 14" tall seated on rocker

EDITION: OOAK

CIRCA: 1999

COLLECTION: American Heartland

MEDIUM: Cernit

FINDINGS: glass eyes, human hair eyelashes, natural human hair wig

ACCESSORIES: two vintage souvenir dolls, wicker rocker

Little Holy Bear

Ute

The Ute tribe's home is in the Great Basin region of the United States between the Sierra Nevada and Wasatch Range. It includes most of Nevada, parts of California, Idaho, Northeastern Utah, Wyoming, and Oregon.

This magnificent Ute native-made pale deerskin cradle board has accented native beaded banding that showcases the artistry of the Ute tribe or nation. A finely beaded turtle amulet is suspended from the cradle's bonnet.

Historically, it holds the baby's umbilical cord and has spiritual powers for ensuring the baby a long life.

Baby holds a sterling silver Sioux rattle inscribed with mythological tribe symbols.

PHOTO: Will Gallie

SIZE: 28" lifesize

EDITION: OOAK

CIRCA: 2000

COLLECTION: Born in America

MEDIUM: Cernit

FINDINGS: human hair eyelashes, fur wig

ACCESSORIES: sterling silver Sioux rattle, beaded turtle amulet, and red fox

A red fox watches over this peacefully sleeping baby.

97

Cheyenne's exceptional fully beaded cradle board was purchased from an American Indian art dealer here in Southern California. When I first saw it at a Glendale, California, Native American art show, I was mesmerized by the craftsmanship, and I especially liked the American flag motif.

Documentation states that it was beaded and created by native artist Louise Tenkiller of Elk City, Oklahoma, sometime between 1970 and 1990.

The cradle was lined with a supple burgundy colored wool trade cloth. Enough fabric was provided to allow for a matching garment to be custom-made for the infant.

The turtle amulet that is suspended from the cradle board traditionally holds baby's umbilical cord and is believed to hold spiritual significance.

Cheyenne

Cheyenne

Cheyenne was sold to a collector of American Indian Art in Santa Fe, New Mexico, during her debut at an art show there.

Weeks later, I delivered the cradle board doll to the collector's lovely Santa Fe style home and saw how beautifully Cheyenne fit into her art collection. Cheyenne was prominently placed next to the woman's favorite easy chair.

Later, the collector reported to me that Cheyenne's spirit took on a noticeable and welcoming human presence in her home. It was apparently felt by all who visited.

PHOTO: Joe Darin

SIZE: lifesize in cradle board

EDITION: OOAK

CIRCA: 2003

COLLECTION: Born in America

MEDIUM: Cernit

FINDINGS: glass eyes, human hair eyelashes, fur wig

ACCESSORIES: beaded reptile amulet, sterling silver earrings and bracelet, sculpted corn

99

Sister Mary, of the order of Sisters of the Holy Cross, is barefoot in a field of wildflowers.

When I was a young fashion designer and pattern maker, one of my sample makers or sewers asked a favor of me. She asked me to visit her church's convent in Los Angeles with her and assist the nuns with making patterns for their religious garments or habits. Apparently, it was a church policy for them to sew their own religious apparel.

It was a marvelous experience, and ultimately I was able to help five or six of them who had varying body types. Custom patterns were made to accommodate each. A couple of the nuns had never sewn before, so I made the patterns as understandable as possible, and offered sewing tips to facilitate the project.

Sister Mary

Sisters of the Holy Cross

Sister Mary of the order of Sisters of the Holy Cross wears a black rayon-and-silk-crepe dress, chiffon trail, starched white cotton bib, and a permanently pleated headpiece. The fluted headpiece was professionally pleated by one of my garment business suppliers in Los Angeles.

She was my very first one-of-a-kind polymer clay sculpted doll. I wasn't sure what she would look like when I started sculpting her, but soon she took on a life of her own. Her serene countenance made me think that she would be a perfect nun.

I first showed her at the New York Toy Fair in 1998, along with four other dolls I had sculpted, but they were of porcelain and made from molds.

She was a favorite of both the curator of the National Museum of Catholic Art and History in NY, and actress Demi Moore. Both ladies wanted to purchase her, but I ended up declining both sales.

I was a new sculptor and was unfamiliar with polymer clays. Super Sculpey was the medium I used, but learned that it may not have been the best choice for a large doll like Sister Mary. The cured clay wasn't as durable as I had expected. Perhaps I did not fire it long enough, or condition it adequately. In any event, she was an early learning experience, and she remains here in my workshop.

PHOTO: Will Gallie

SIZE: approximately 24" tall

EDITION: OOAK

CIRCA: 1998

COLLECTION: Religions of the World

MEDIUM: Super Sculpey

FINDINGS: glass eyes, human hair eyelashes; no wig

ACCESSORIES: St. Christopher medal, rosary, faux field flowers

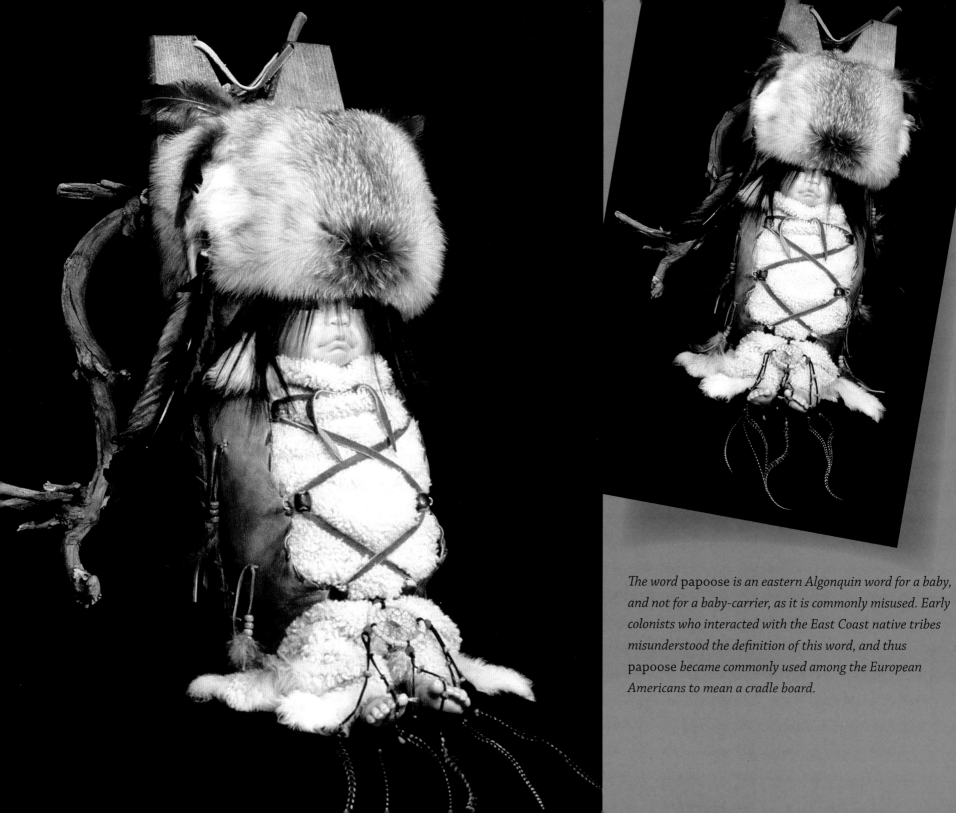

The word papoose *is an eastern Algonquin word for a baby, and not for a baby-carrier, as it is commonly misused. Early colonists who interacted with the East Coast native tribes misunderstood the definition of this word, and thus* papoose *became commonly used among the European Americans to mean a cradle board.*

Kicking Bear

Pueblo

Kicking Bear is swaddled in lambswool sherpa in his native-made Pueblo cradle board. In many ways, the cradle resembles those of the Navajo.

The wood cradle is made from deer hide and is adorned with turquoise beads, feathers, and a dream catcher. A giant red fox towers over baby as a part of the cradle board.

Here, the cradle leans agains a twig.

PHOTO: Lynn Cartwright

SIZE: 30" tall

EDITION: OOAK

CIRCA: 2004

COLLECTION: Born in America

MEDIUM: Cernit

ACCESSORIES: Pueblo cradle board

Danny

Christening Baby

Often little boys look very much like little girls, especially when they wear christening dresses. This is true in Danny's case. Here is a lovely portraiture of Danny in his special gown, wearing a light blue sweater and beret to complement his baby-blue eyes.

The long heirloom christening dress is antique and was purchased from a San Francisco specialty antique dealer. There is a Victorian crystal teething charm suspended on a satin ribbon around Danny's neck. A vintage Humpty Dumpty rattle offers to be a good companion.

Even Danny's distressed old chair coordinates nicely in light blue to complete his boyish statement.

PHOTO: Will Gallie

SIZE: approximately 31" seated on chair

EDITION: OOAK

CIRCA: 2002

COLLECTION: Religions of the World

MEDIUM: Cernit

FINDINGS: glass eyes, human hair eyelashes

ACCESSORIES: a Victorian teething charm, vintage Humpty Dumpty, and a distressed light blue wooden chair

Juneau enjoys the magnificent Alaska winter.

Juneau & Baby Harp Seal

Inuit

Juneau wears warm winter furs over a wool hand-knit sweater by the artist. Her lambskin and sherpa parka is dramatically accented with voluptuous fox fur. The fox fur softly frames baby's sweet face.

Her leggings are warm bunny fur.

The tundra boots are predominantly fur with partially sculpted areas to resemble classic Inuit snow boots.

The baby harp seal is Juneau's cherished companion.

PHOTO: Lynn Cartwright

SIZE: 20" tall

EDITION: OOAK

CIRCA: 2006

COLLECTION: Born in America

MEDIUM: Pro-Sculpt

FINDINGS: glass eyes, fur wig, human hair eyelashes

ACCESSORIES: rabbit fur baby harp seal

Background image courtesy of Faber Snowshoes-Raquettes

Chir'r'y

Hupa/Modoc/Yurok

Here is an outstanding example of the typical basketry of the Hupa/Modoc/Yurok tribes of northwestern California and the Oregon border region. Both the cradle basket and cap are authentic native-made from local grasses.

Chir'r'y's ceremonial cap is artfully woven into a geometric pattern using *tule,* a bulrush or cattail plant that grows abundantly in marshy areas of California. Dried porcupine quills add additional design elements as well as structural stability to the piece.

PHOTO: Will Gallie

SIZE: 30" cradle length

EDITION: OOAK

CIRCA: 2009

COLLECTION: Born in America

MEDIUM: ProSculpt

FINDINGS: glass eyes, human hair eyelashes, fur hair

ACCESSORIES: sculpted corn cobs and acorns

Sculpted acorns and corn cobs adorn the baby's cradle as a wish for long life and abundance. Both of these foods are vital to the northern California tribes.

Acorns are used in mush, bread, pancakes, and the like as an important food source. Corn, too, is a basic nutritional foodstuff.

Chir'r'y is swaddled in cotton gauze in typical native manner in the cradle. Local straws and grasses line the base of the cradle basket, since there were no Pampers available back then.

Chir'r'y is accessorized with sterling silver jewelry, beaded moccasins, and of course, this wonderful high quality ceremonial cap.

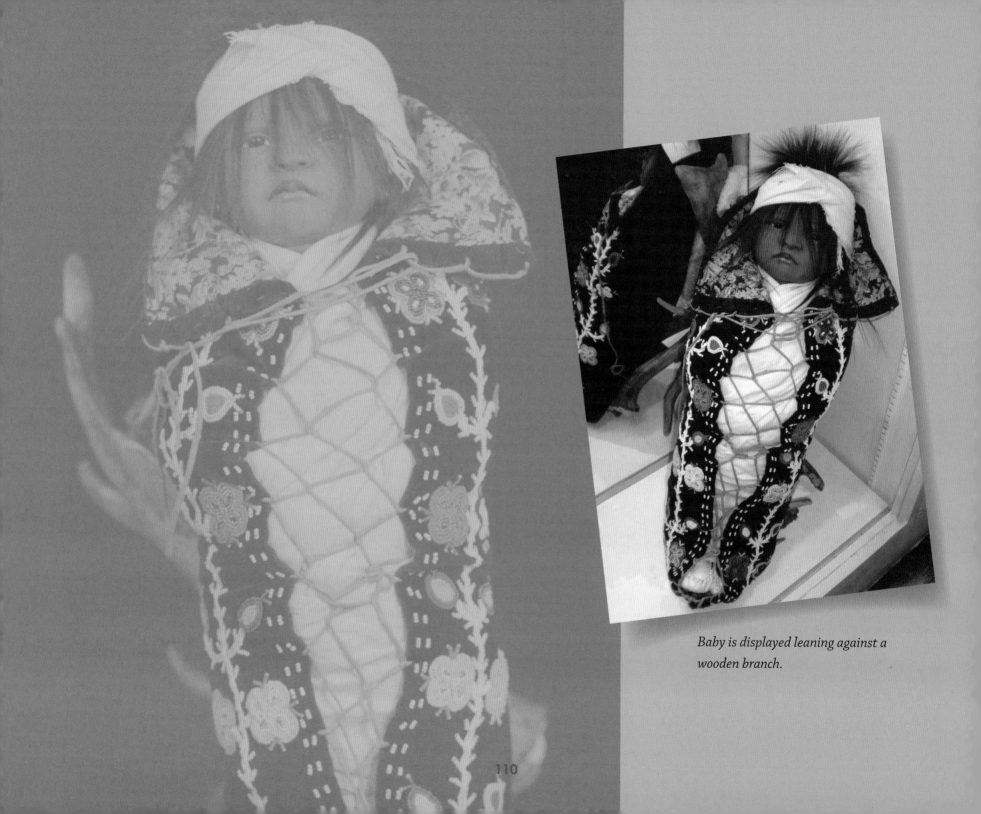

Baby is displayed leaning against a
wooden branch.

110

Golden Flower

James Bay Cree

Baby is securely wrapped in a vintage James Bay Cree soft cradle bundle. The floral design is beaded on a black velvet ground and is characteristic of the Cree artistry circa the 1930s.

This beautiful native cradle originated in a private collection out of Banff, Alberta, Canada, prior to my purchasing it in auction. A major portion of the Cree nation resides in Canada, north and west of Lake Superior, in Ontario, Manitoba, Saskatchewan, Alberta, Quebec, and the Northwest Territories.

Golden Flower is in her soft cradle bundle now, but I am on a quest for a Cree cedar wood cradle back board to complete her image.

PHOTO: Lynn Cartwright

SIZE: 24"

EDITION: OOAK

CIRCA: 2009

COLLECTION: Born in America

MEDIUM: Pro-Sculpt

FINDINGS: glass eyes, human hair eyelashes, fur wig

ACCESSORIES: James Bay Cree soft cradle

Anika wears a wreath of faux evergreen boughs and sculpted candles, and a traditional long white dress with a red ribbon sash.

She holds a saffron Swedish Lussekatter or S-shaped Swedish holiday bun pastry.

On December 13th, the tradition is for the eldest daughter in the family to awaken her parents with this delightful Swedish pastry.

Anika cannot resist taking a nibble for herself!

Anika, Santa Lucia

Sweden

December 13th is the beginning of the Scandinavian Winter Solstice. To celebrate, a magical ceremony takes place that originated in Sweden around the year 304 AD.

The candlelit ceremony came about as a result of the stories told by monks who first brought Christianity to Sweden. Santa Lucia was a young Christian girl who was martyred for her faith. She had secretly brought food to persecuted Christians in Rome who were in hiding in catacombs under the city. She wore candles in her hair in order to free up her hands to carry the food. The name *Lucia* means light.

PHOTO: Lynn Cartwright

SIZE: 27"

EDITION: OOAK

CIRCA: 2004

COLLECTION: One World

MEDIUM: Cernit

FINDINGS: glass eyes, human hair wig

ACCESSORIES: faux evergreen boughs, sculpted candles, sculpted Swedish holiday bun

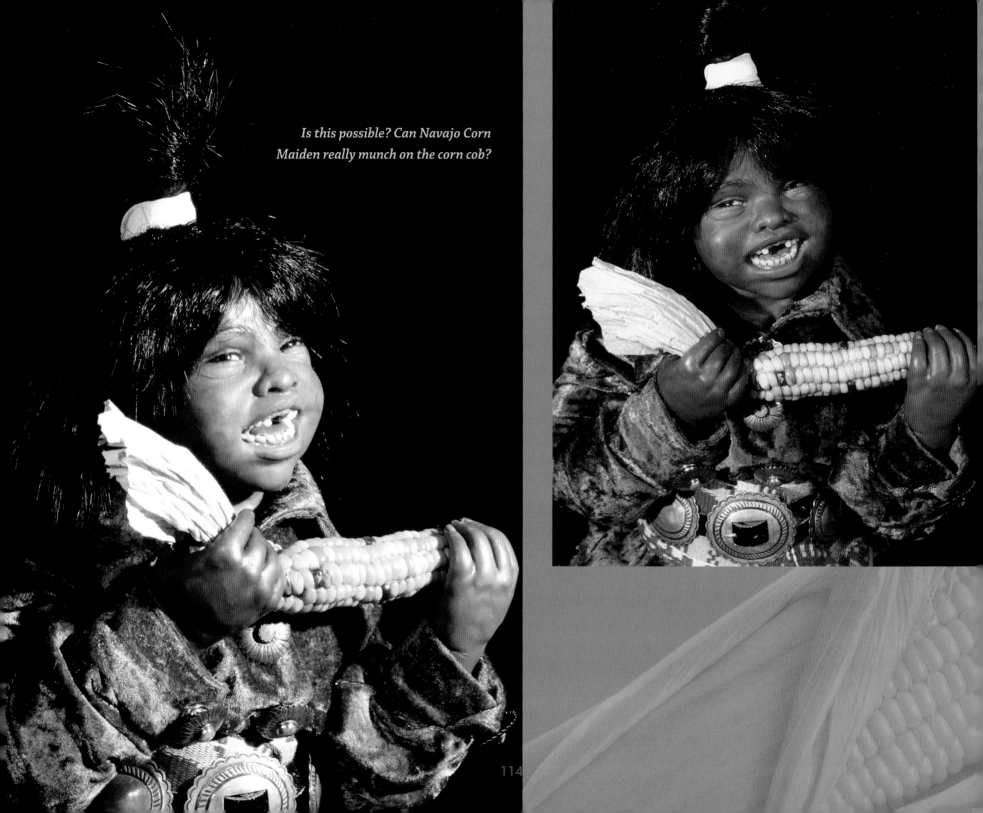

Is this possible? Can Navajo Corn Maiden really munch on the corn cob?

114

Navajo Corn Maiden

Navajo velvet has enduring timeless beauty. It is cleverly shown here in a traditionally styled blouse over a classic Navajo tiered prairie skirt.

Sterling silver and turquoise buttons punctuate the blouse and nicely coordinate with a classic silver conch belt.

The hand-woven waist sash is native-made and makes a colorful backdrop for the silver conch belt.

Navajo Corn Maiden's hide moccasins with side silver buttons are sculpted to replicate classic Navajo short boots.

PHOTO: Will Gallie

SIZE: 19½" seated height

EDITION: OOAK

CIRCA: uncertain

COLLECTION: Born in America

MEDIUM: Cernit

FINDINGS: glass eyes, human hair eyelashes, synthetic hair wig

ACCESSORIES: silver conch belt, turquoise and silver buttons and jewelry,
   sculpted corn cobs

Anne & Dolly

Both Anne and Dolly are dressed in retro-style, turn-of-the-nineteenth-century garments. Anne's powder blue sweater was hand-knit by the artist and edged with a French silk embroidered ribbon that accents her auburn hair. Her white lingerie dress, as it was called then, is antique and has a hand-made lace border.

Her black crochet cloche is laden with blue silk ribbon rosettes matching her light blue hand-knit sweater.

Anne's high top shoes are artfully hand-sculpted and meticulously laced with leather tongs to rival the real thing. Shoes like this were typical of the time.

Dolly, her companion doll, is also made to look antique, as if Anne's grandmother had passed down this heirloom. Note the masculine way of crossing the collar: left over right. This was the norm in eighteenth-century Europe. Today, the style is to cross right over left for females.

PHOTO: Will Gallie

SIZE: 19½" seated height

EDITION: OOAK

CIRCA: 2000

COLLECTION: American Heartland

MEDIUM: Anne- ProSculpt; Dolly is in an air-dry clay

FINDINGS: glass eyes, human hair eyelashes, human hair wig; companion doll has mohair wig

ACCESSORIES: antique jewelry, hand-crafted cloche hat with silk rosebuds, sculpted high top shoes

A story of tribute to a fine doll artist...

Anne & Dolly is a dual sculpture. Both Anne and her companion doll are hand-sculpted by the artist. Anne was originally inspired by famous contemporary Parisienne one-of-a-kind doll maker/sculptor Anne Mitrani.

Mitrani is known for sculpting primarily redheaded dolls peppered with freckles. She is widely acknowledged as being a forerunner of the contemporary Original Artist Doll movement. Her dolls have been known to sell for an astounding $20,000 each!

Her unique work is remarkable, and that's truly an understatement. This is my salute to Anne Mitrani, an important and remarkable contemporary doll artist.

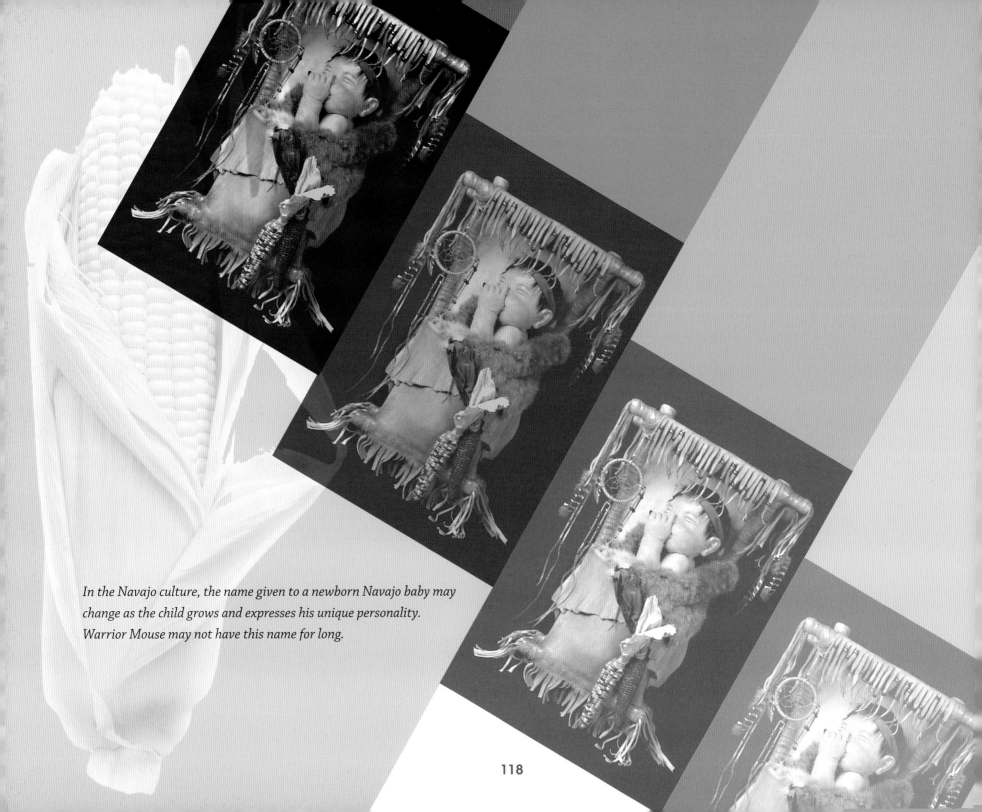

In the Navajo culture, the name given to a newborn Navajo baby may change as the child grows and expresses his unique personality. Warrior Mouse may not have this name for long.

118

Warrior Mouse

Navajo

Warrior Mouse sleeps in a fur-lined Navajo cradle board that is hand-crafted of Arizona desert cactus ribs, and tanned deer hide. The cradle was made by Arizona Navajo artists cleverly calling themselves the Buffalo Gals.

Colorful sculpted corn cobs are suspended from the cradle and represent a wish for prosperity and abundance in baby's life, while a native-made dream catcher wards off evil spirits and restores sweet dreams.

PHOTO: Will Gallie

SIZE: 21" cradle board length

EDITION: OOAK

CIRCA: 2003

COLLECTION: Born in America

MEDIUM: Cernit

FINDINGS: fur hair, human hair eyelashes

ACCESSORIES: feathers, dream catcher, Navajo cradle, sculpted corn

Warrior Mouse sleeps serenely surrounded by autumn shades of hand-sculpted native corn that are a wish for lifelong abundance.

Zola

Africa

Plump-cheeked Zola is a typical kid with a rag doll baby in tow, kangaroo-style.

Her zany human hair natural do is accented with bold black-and-white hand-made African trade beads.

Her raw silk burlap ensemble is cinched at the waist with a colorful Nigerian woven wrap. Tucked in her waistband is a marvelous antique black rag doll, which is wondrous in itself.

What I like most about Zola is her stylized ethnic look, and that her delightful hair is actually real human hair.

PHOTO: Jennifer Cartwright

SIZE: 28" tall

EDITION: OOAK

CIRCA: 2008

COLLECTION: One World

MEDIUM: Cernit

FINDINGS: glass eyes, human hair wig, human hair eyelashes

ACCESSORIES: antique black rag doll, African trade beads

Appendix

Favorite Vendors, Suppliers, and Contacts

Air Lite Manufacturing, Inc.
www.airlitemanufacturing.com
Email: e.herman@airlitemanufacturing.com
(800) 521-1267; (248) 335-8131
Pontiac, MI 48341
Bulk fiberfill manufacturer of "cluster fiberfill"

Amaco/Brent
www.amaco.com
Email: salessupport@amaco.com
(800) 374-1600; (317) 244-6871
Clay crafting machine, aka pasta machine

Amazon Handmade
www.amazon.com
A marketing website for global artists; must meet certain standards

AT Enterprises
Fred MacNeil
www.atenterprises.com
Email: fredmacneil@yahoo.com
(951) 264-3830
PO Box 2024
Corona, CA 92878
High quality custom acrylic showcases; will ship

Cartwright, Lynn
www.lynncartwrightdolls.com or www.originalartistdolls.com
Email: dolldesigner@yahoo.com or lynn@originalartistdolls.com
(661) 706-5467
3501 Mall View Rd, Ste 115-248
Bakersfield, CA 93306
Author, doll maker

Central Shippee, Inc.
www.thefeltpeople.com
Email: feltlucy@optonline.net
(800) 631-8968; (973) 838-1100
Bloomingdale, NJ 07403
Premiere 14 and 16 oz. wool felt for doll body/torso; color match to skin tone; wide color selection

Children of the Heart
www.childrenoftheheart.net
Email: susan@childrenoftheheart.net
(517) 575-0015
Susan Anderson
Seasoned original artist doll sales agent; global clientele

Clay Factory, Inc. aka Clay Factory of Escondido
www.clayfactoryinc.com
Email: info@clayfactory.net
(760) 741-3242
Howard Segal
Escondido, CA 92046
Cernit and polymer clay supplier

CR's Crafts

www.crscraft.com

Email: crservice@crscraft.com

(641) 567-3652

Leland, IA 50453

Plastic beaded armature supplier by the foot or running yards

Dick Blick Art Materials

www.dickblick.com

(877) 714- 4159

Sennelier French oil paints, general art supplies

Dollery, The

www.dollery.com

Email: kmalone@dollery.com

(781) 447-6677

Whitman, MA 02382

Kim Malone

Seasoned original artist doll sales agent; global clientele

Etsy

www.etsy.com

Popular online website venue for artists; reasonable sales fees

Fred Segal retail store

www.fredsegal.com

Email: info@fredsegal.com

(310) 394-1875

420 Broadway

Santa Monica, CA

Trendy upscale Southern California boutique

G. Schoepfer Inc. Eyes for Dolls

www.schoepferseyes.com

Email: amy@schoepferseyes.com

(800) 875-6939; (203) 250-7794

Amy Schoepfer

Glass doll eyes; great library of choices; antique and hard-to-find eyes

Gustav Adolf Dietz

www.dollpoint.de

Email: info@dollpoint.de

+49 (0) 761-35960

Online shopping for German glass eyes, eyelashes, etc.

His and Her Hair

www.hisandhers.com

(800) 421- 4417; (323) 931-1021

Email: info@hisandher.com

5525 Wilshire Blvd

Los Angeles, CA 90036

Largest supply of hair for wig making imaginable; services the motion picture industry

Lauscher German-made Glass Doll Eyes

www.dollsbysandie.com (US representative)

Quality European glass doll eyes

Michaels Craft Stores

www.michaels.com

Consult your local directory

Poly pellets, fiberfill, misc. supplies, etc.

NEVERknead

www.neverknead.com

Email: neverknead@gmail.com

(323) 640-0003

Highland Park, CA

Quality polymer clay conditioning press

Polymer Clayer

www.polymerclayer.com

Email: through website

(619) 800-1999

Nancy Ulrich

El Cajon, CA 92020

Great tried-and-true tips on polymer clay crafting

Professional Doll Makers Art Guild (PDMAG)

www.artdollguild.com

Email: PDMAGuild@gmail.com;

Jack Johnston, jack@artdolls.com

(801) 510-3006; (727) 224-2509

Doll makers guild association; provides classes

Yesterware Restorations

Email: yesterware@bak.rr.com

(661) 322-2837

A great resource for quality ceramic, etc., repairs; ships

Bibliography

Brettar, Martine. *Kinder-anatomie.* 2000.
This is an excellent reference book on child anatomy for artists and sculptors.

Clark, Roberta Carter. *How to Paint Living Portraits.* Cincinnati: North Light Books, 1990.
Even though this book targets painters and illustrators, it has great value for doll sculptors, too. I especially think that the chapters on the anatomy of heads and on body proportions are helpful. The author addresses various ages.

Cooper, James. "Christmas in Sweden." http://whychristmas.com.
This informative article is on the St. Lucia Day traditional holiday ceremony.

DeVoto, Jeanne A.E. "The Polymer ClaySpot." http://jaedworks.com
This website offers a wealth of knowledge on polymer clay crafting plus online help.

Faigin, Gary. *The Artist's Complete Guide to Facial Expressions.* New York: Watson- Guptill Publications, 1990.
This book is a must to add to your reference library. The facial expressions illustrated are right on target.

Goldfinger, Eliot. *Human Anatomy for Artists.* New York: Oxford University Press, 1991.
The hyper-realistic illustrations make it an ideal reference book for sculptors of realism.

Henry, Pat. *FDQ: In Focus, Digital Photography for the Doll Collector.* New York: FDQ Media, Inc., 2009.
This book divulges little-known techniques and equipment used by doll industry professionals.

Landau, Elizabeth. "Chart" (blog). "Why our noses are different shapes." March 20, 2013. http://thechart.blogs.cnn.com/2013/03/20/why-our-noses-are-different-shapes/
This is an interesting article on noses.

Lindgren, Astrid. *Pippi Longstocking.* Translated by Florence Lamborn. Stockholm: Raben & Sjogren, 1945.
This is the original story about Pippi Longstocking that started it all.

National Geographic, 2016. "Harp Seal." Photographs by Cassandra D., Your Shot. http://www.nationalgeographic.com/animals/mammals/h/harp-seal/.
This is an educational article dedicated to harp seals.

Native Languages of the Americas. "Native American Cradleboards." Contacts and FAQ page, 1998-2015. http://native-languages.org.

Oliver, Georgina. "Is This Kid for Real? Artist Anne Mitrani's Dolls Can Fool You Even in The, Er, Flesh." *People,* vol. 32 no. 22, Nov. 27, 1989. http://people.com.

Rand, Ayn. *The Romantic Manifesto.* New York: Harry N. Abrams, Inc. & Penguin Putnam, Inc., 1975.
This is an objective and philosophical analysis of art.

SculptureHouse, Inc. http://sculpturehouse.com.
This website offers broad and informative material on polymer clay crafting.

Shepherd's Conservation Society. "Harp Seals May Be Extinct in Two Decades. October 29, 2006. http://seashepherd.org.

Index

The realistically compelling artist dolls of **Lynn Cartwright** celebrate diverse cultures and ethnicities. Her meticulously handmade dolls include commissioned portrait dolls, character dolls, and dolls that make a broader contemporary social statement. The authentic detail in her work elevates it to a museum-quality standard.

Her career in fashion design, spanning more than four decades, accidentally led to her second career in doll making. In the world of fashion design Cartwright made innovative strides in activewear, swimwear, lifestyle sportswear, athletic footwear, and uniforms. Her warmhearted textile prints revolutionized nurses' scrubs in the 1990s. Designing the US gymnastics team's Olympic uniforms (1984, 1988) was Cartwright's most prestigious undertaking; recall Mary Lou Retton! Doll making is the perfect reflection of Cartwright's autobiography, combining fashion design, art, and travel experiences.

She has won six DOTY (Doll of the Year) Industry Awards, the DOTY Public Award, two Diamond Industry Awards of Excellence, five Apex Award nominations, and other accolades.

Visit her on Facebook, Etsy, and at www.lynncartwrightdolls.com.